PRINCE2® 2009 EDITI

D0868580

Other publications by Van Haren Publishing

Van Haren Publishing (VHP) specializes in titles on Best Practices, methods and standards within four domains:

- IT and IT Management
- Architecture (Enterprise and IT)
- Business management and
- Project management

Van Haren Publishing offers a wide collection of whitepapers, templates, free e-books, trainer material etc. in the **Van Haren Publishing Knowledge Base**: www.vanharen.net for more details.

Van Haren Publishing is also publishing on behalf of leading organizations and companies: ASLBiSL Foundation, CA, Centre Henri Tudor, Gaming Works, IACCM, IAOP, IPMA-NL, ITSqc, NAF, Ngi, PMI-NL, PON, The Open Group, The SOX Institute.

Topics are (per domain):

IT and IT Management	**Architecture (Enterprise and IT)**	**Project Management**
ABC of ICT	Archimate®	A4-Projectmanagement
ASL®	BIP / Novius	ICB / NCB
CATS CM®	GEA®	MINCE®
CMMI®	TOGAF®	M_o_R®
CoBIT		MSP™
Frameworx	**Business Management**	P3O®
ISO 17799	BiSL®	*PMBOK® Guide*
ISO 27001	Contract Management	PRINCE2®
ISO 27002	EFQM	
ISO/IEC 20000	eSCM	
ISPL	ISA-95	
IT Service CMM	ISO 9000	
ITIL®	ISO 9001:2000	
MOF	OPBOK	
MSF	SAP	
SABSA	SixSigma	
	SOX	
	SqEME®	

PRINCE2® 2009 Edition
Edition
A Pocket Guide

Bert Hedeman
Ron Seegers

Licensed Product

Colophon

Title:	PRINCE2® 2009 Edition – A Pocket Guide
Series:	Best Practice
Authors:	Bert Hedeman, Ron Seegers
Reviewers:	Ernst Bosschers (ISES International)
	Arthur Coppens (Getronics)
	Francisca Kouwen (Getronics)
	Mark Kouwenhoven (PMcoaching)
	Joost Nuyten (Rabobank)
	Arie den Ouden (Ambidexter Management)
Text editor:	Steve Newton
Publisher:	Van Haren Publishing, Zaltbommel,
	ww.vanharen.net
ISBN:	978 90 8753 544 5
Print:	First edition, first impression, September 2009
	First edition, second impression, November 2009
	First edition, third impression, August 2010
	First edition, fourth impression, September 2012
Layout and type setting:	CO2 Premedia, Amersfoort – NL
Copyright:	© Van Haren Publishing, 2009

Contents

1	**Introduction**	**1**
1.1	The purpose of this guide	1
1.2	What is a project?	1
1.3	Why are projects important?	2
1.4	What makes a project different from regular business?	2
1.5	What is project management?	3
1.6	What does a Project Manager do?	4
1.7	What is it all parties involved wish to control?	5

2	**Introduction to PRINCE2**	**7**
2.1	Structure of PRINCE2	8
2.2	Related OGC guidance	9
2.3	What PRINCE2 does not provide	10
2.4	Benefits of PRINCE2	11
2.5	How to use this pocket guide	12

3	**PRINCE2 2009 Edition versus 2005 Edition**	**13**
3.1	Main structural changes	13
3.2	Changes to the manual	14
3.3	Detailed changes	14

4	**Principles**	**19**
4.1	Continued business justification	19
4.2	Learn from experience	20
4.3	Defined roles and responsibilities	20
4.4	Manage by stages	21
4.5	Manage by exception	21
4.6	Focus on products	22
4.7	Tailor to suit the project environment	22

5	**Introduction to PRINCE2 Themes**	**23**

6	**Business Case**	**25**
6.1	Purpose	25
6.2	Business Case defined	25
6.3	PRINCE2 approach to Business Case	26
6.4	The contents of a Business Case	28
6.5	Responsibilities of the Business Case theme	30

7	**Organization**	**31**
7.1	Purpose	31
7.2	Organization defined	31
7.3	Levels of organization	32
7.4	Project management team	34
7.5	Communication Management Strategy	37

8	**Quality**	**39**
8.1	Purpose	39
8.2	Quality definitions	39
8.3	Quality management	40
8.4	PRINCE2 approach to quality	42
8.5	Responsibilities of the Quality theme	44

9	**Plans**	**45**
9.1	Purpose	45
9.2	Plans defined	45
9.3	PRINCE2 approach to plans	47
9.4	Product-based planning technique	48
9.5	Responsibilities of the Plans theme	51

10	**Risks**	**53**
10.1	Purpose	53
10.2	Risk defined	53
10.3	Risk Management Strategy	54
10.4	Risk Register	54
10.5	Risk management procedures	55
10.6	Responsibilities of the Risk theme	59

11	**Change**	**61**
11.1	Purpose	61
11.2	Change defined	61
11.3	PRINCE2 approach to Change	62
11.4	Configuration Management procedure	64
11.5	Issue and change control procedure	65
11.6	Responsibilities of the Change theme	67

12	**Progress**	**69**
12.1	Purpose	69
12.2	Progress defined	69
12.3	Management by Exception	70

12.4   PRINCE2 approach to Progress   70
12.5   Delegating authority   70
12.6   Management stages   72
12.7   Event- and time-driven controls   73
12.8   Raising exceptions   75
12.9   Responsibilities of the Progress theme   76

13   Introduction to PRINCE2 processes   77
13.1   Pre-project   78
13.2   Initiation stage   79
13.3   Subsequent delivery stage(s)   79
13.4   Final delivery stage   79

14   Starting up a Project   81
14.1   Purpose   81
14.2   Objectives   82
14.3   Context   82
14.4   Activities and recommended actions   82

15   Directing a Project   87
15.1   Purpose   87
15.2   Objectives   87
15.3   Context   88
15.4   Activities and recommended actions   88

16   Initiating a Project   91
16.1   Purpose   91
16.2   Objectives   91
16.3   Context   92
16.4   Activities and recommended actions   92

17   Controlling a Stage   97
17.1   Purpose   97
17.2   Objectives   97
17.3   Context   98
17.4   Activities and recommended actions   98

18   Managing Product Delivery   103
18.1   Purpose   103
18.2   Objectives   103
18.3   Context   104
18.4   Activities and recommended actions   104

19	**Managing a Stage Boundary**	**107**
19.1	Purpose	107
19.2	Objectives	108
19.3	Context	108
19.4	Activities and recommended actions	108

20	**Closing a Project**	**113**
20.1	Purpose	113
20.2	Objectives	114
20.3	Context	114
20.4	Activities and recommended actions	115

21	**Tailoring PRINCE2**	**119**
21.1	What is tailoring?	119
21.2	General approach to tailoring	120
21.3	Examples of tailoring	121
21.4	Projects in a programme environment	121
21.5	Project scale	124
21.6	Commercial customer/supplier environment	126
21.7	Multi-organization projects	128
21.8	Project type	128
21.9	Sector differences	130
21.10	Bodies of Knowledge	130

Appendix A - Outline Product Descriptions for the management products — **133**
Appendix B - Roles and responsibilities — **151**
Appendix C - Example of product-based planning — **159**
Appendix D - Glossary — **162**
Appendix E - Governance — **182**
Appendix F - Organizations — **183**
Appendix G - References — **184**
About the authors — **184**

Chapter 1
Introduction

PRINCE2® is a generic project management method which focuses on the management aspects of projects. PRINCE2® was originally launched in 1996 by the CCTA. Since then several versions have been launched. The newest update of the method has been published in June 2009.

PRINCE2® is now a registered trade mark of the Office of Government Commerce (OGC) in the United Kingdom and other countries. The APM Group Limited (APMG) has been licensed to provide certification to organizations, activities and persons related (but not limited to) projects, programmes and risk based on the methods developed by the British Government. These are managed from the company's UK head office, with the operational activities being provided through APMG's subsidiary offices.

1.1   The purpose of this guide

This pocket guide supplies a summary of the PRINCE2 method. It is intended to provide a quick introduction as well as a structured overview of the method and to act as a reference for those who have studied the method in the past and want to use the method now in the day-to-day management of their projects.

1.2   What is a project?

A project is a set of related activities within a temporary organization that is created to deliver, according to agreed conditions, one or more predefined products or services.

Within the context of the method of PRINCE2 a project is defined as:

> A temporary organization that is created for the purpose of delivering
> one or more business products according to an agreed Business Case.

1.3   Why are projects important?

Projects are mainly carried out under conditions where normal business
operations cannot deliver properly. One of these conditions is when the
business operations have to transform to meet new requirements, in order
to survive or to compete in the future.

The temporary organization of projects makes it possible to bring all
stakeholders together to deliver the required products or services. The
structure and processes within a proper project management method
enforce focus, support and commitment for the products and services that
are to be delivered. Projects are therefore an important means to support
change.

As business change is becoming more and more important in the present
governmental activities and business operations, projects nowadays are
crucial in professional life.

1.4   What makes a project different from regular business?

Based on the definition of a project, there are a number of characteristics of
projects that distinguish project work from regular business operations:

Change – most projects are carried out in a changing environment and are, at the same time, the means by which the organization introduces these changes. This will often cause severe resistance from the parties involved. The project has to manage this resistance and, increasingly, has to contribute in diminishing this resistance in addition to also meeting its requirements in terms of delivering the predefined products and services.

Temporary – this is an essential condition for a project. Without this, there is no project. A project ends automatically when the predefined products or services are handed over to the customer. Projects by nature are finite, they have a predefined start and end.

Cross-functional – projects involve a team of people with different skills and functions, most often from different organizational entities. This can be from within a single organization or from several organizations.

Unique – every project is different, even when an identical product or service is delivered. The context is always different and there are always differences in objectives, new team members or other parties involved. This makes each project unique in relation to every other project.

Uncertainty – all the characteristics above result in uncertainty and this will always introduce opportunities and threats. You cannot exclude this, you only can manage it. Projects are typically more risky than the normal business operations. Management of risk (uncertainty) is therefore at the core of project management.

1.5   What is project management?

Project management is the planning, delegation, monitoring and control of all aspects of the project, and the motivation of those involved, to achieve the project objectives within the expected performance targets for time, cost, quality, scope, benefits and risks, see figure 1.1.

Figure 1.1 Project management cycle (Source: Managing Successful Projects with PRINCE2, produced by OGC)

The purpose of project management is to keep control over the specialist work required to create the project's products.

Project management, therefore, within this definition is not limited to the work of the Project Manager. Project management is a duty of all involved in the management of the project. This includes the Executive, the members of the Project Board, the Project Manager and the respective Team Managers.

1.6   What does a Project Manager do?

The Project Manager is responsible for the day-to-day management of the project, within the directions set by the Executive/Project Board.

As part of this day-to-day management, the Project Manager is responsible for the planning, delegation, monitoring and control of the works to be carried out, as well as for the management of other aspects of the project, such as:

- Engagement of stakeholders to create support and commitment and to diminish resistance;
- Planning and monitoring of the benefits to be achieved in the customer organization through the project output;
- Motivation of team members and all who are contributing to the project.

1.7   What is it all parties involved wish to control?

There are considered to be six basic aspects involved in any project:

Costs – the costs involved to create the defined project products. This also includes the costs to manage the project.

Time – the total lifecycle of the project and/or the date of handing over the project products.

Quality – the product's ability to meet its requirements.

Scope – what is included in the project product? What has to be delivered and what not? What work has to be carried out and what not?

Risks - the management of threats as well as the management of the opportunities.

Benefits – the benefits to be realized based on the project's output.

In addition to these basic aspects, other aspects are often involved in projects, such as health, environment, safety and security, together with issues such as support and commitment.

Chapter 2
Introduction to PRINCE2

PRINCE2 is a structured project management method, based on best practice.

PRINCE2 is a non-proprietary method. Project Managers and others are free to use the method in their own practice.

PRINCE2 is truly generic. It can be applied to any project, regardless of scale, type, organization, geography or culture. However the method always has to be tailored to the project in hand.

PRINCE2 achieves this by isolating the management aspects of project work from the specialist contributions, such as design, construction, etc. However the specialist work can easily be integrated with the PRINCE2 method.

Because PRINCE2 is generic and based on proven principles, organizations can easily adopt the method as a standard and substantially improve their organizational capability to perform projects and deliver change.

PRINCE2 is protected by trademark. Professional training is restricted to Accredited Training Organizations and their Affiliates. See the websites of the APMG and its subsidiary offices.

2.1   Structure of PRINCE2

The PRINCE2 method addresses project management from four different perspectives, see figure 2.1:

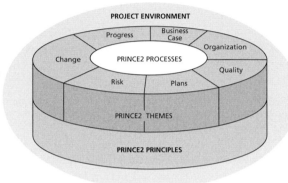

Figure 2.1 The structure of PRINCE2™ (Source: Managing Successful Projects with PRINCE2, produced by OGC)

1. **Seven Principles** – these are the guiding obligations and good practices which determine whether the project is genuinely being managed using PRINCE2. Unless all of them are applied, a project it is not considered a PRINCE2 project.
2. **Seven Themes** – these describe the aspects of project management that must be addressed continually and in parallel throughout the project. The themes explain the specific treatment required by PRINCE2 for various project management disciplines and why they are necessary.
3. **Seven Processes** – these describe a step-wise progression through the project lifecycle. Each process provides checklists of recommended activities, products and related responsibilities.

4. **Tailoring PRINCE2** – this relates to the tailoring of PRINCE2 to the specific context of the project. This context depends on specific project factors as well as environmental factors.

2.2 Related OGC guidance

PRINCE2 is part of a suite of guidance, see figure 2.2, developed by the UK Office of Government Commerce (OGC), which is aimed at helping organizations and individuals manage their projects, programmes and services consistently and effectively.

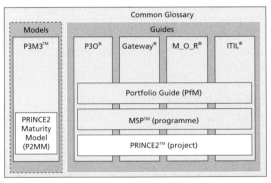

Figure 2.2 OGC Best Practice Guidance (Source: Managing Successful Projects with PRINCE2, produced by OGC)

P3M3™ – Portfolio, Programme and Project Management Maturity Model is a reference guide for structured best practice. It breaks down the broad disciplines of portfolio, programme and project management into hierarchy of Key Process Areas (KPAs). P3M3 distinguishes five maturity levels.

P2MM – PRINCE2 Maturity Model describes a set of KPAs required for the effective implementation and use of PRINCE2 within an organization. P2MM is derived from P3M3.

P3O™ – P3O stands for Portfolio, Programme and Project Office. This framework provides guidance on how to define, establish and operate such an Office (Project Management Office, PMO).

Gateway™ – OGC Gateway Review Process is a well established project and programme assurance review process, which is mandated for all UK Government high-risk programmes and projects.

M_O_R® – Management of Risk puts the management of project risk into the context of the wider business environment.

ITIL® – IT Infrastructure Library provides a cohesive set of best practice guidance for IT service management.

PfM – Portfolio Management Guide explains the key principles of portfolio management.

MSP™ – Managing Successful Programmes – represents proven programme management best practice in successfully delivering transformational change.

2.3   What PRINCE2 does not provide

There are three broad areas which are deliberately outside the scope of PRINCE2:

Specialist work – PRINCE2's strength is in its wide application. Consequently industry-specific or type-specific activities are outside the scope of PRINCE2. However PRINCE2 can easily be aligned to specialist lifecycle models.

Techniques – there are many proven planning and control techniques. Such techniques are well documented elsewhere. Techniques are only included in PRINCE2 where they contribute to the specific PRINCE2 treatment of a theme, e.g. the product-based planning technique for developing plans.

Leadership capability – leadership and other social skills are inherently important in project management but impossible to codify in a method.

Also these are well documented elsewhere. However the principles, themes and processes of PRINCE2 facilitate a good performance of these skills and contribute in this way to the performance of the project too.

2.4   Benefits of PRINCE2

PRINCE2 delivers benefits to all parties concerned, especially the customers, suppliers and the Project Manager. Although most characteristics of PRINCE2 are of benefit to all, a certain sub-division can be made:

- Proven best practice, widely recognized;
- Can be applied to any type of project;
- Provides a common vocabulary and approach;
- Integrates easily with industry-specific standards;

- Allocates resources as part of the go/no-go moments;
- Thorough but economical structure of reports;
- Restricts meetings to only those that are essential;

- Promotes learning and continuous improvement;
- Promotes reuse of project assets, facilitates staff mobility;
- Availability of Accredited Training Organizations;

- Clear roles and responsibilities for all participants;
- Focus on continuous justification of the project;
- Participation of stakeholders in planning and decision making;
- Management by Exception for senior management;

- Product focus: what a project will deliver;
- Plans meet the needs of different levels of management;
- Quality control during whole lifecycle of the project;
- Manages business and project risks;

- Ensures issues are escalated;
- Diagnostic tool for assurance and assessments.

2.5   How to use this pocket guide

Of course this pocket guide can be read from cover to cover. However for those who wish to get a quick introduction to the PRINCE2 method, you are advised to read in particular the introductory chapters (chapters 1 and 2) together with chapter 4 Principles, chapter 5 Overview Themes and chapter 13 Introduction to PRINCE2 Processes.

The senior management of the project are advised to read in addition chapter 15 Directing a Project and chapter 21 Tailoring PRINCE2. For a specific reference the respective chapter can be read in conjunction with the corresponding appendices.

PRINCE2 management products, as defined in appendix A Outline Product Descriptions and appendix C Roles and Responsibilities, are written in the text with a capital for the reader's convenience.

Chapter 3
PRINCE2 2009 Edition versus 2005 Edition

The essential improvement is that PRINCE2 has become much more principle based. PRINCE2 is now much more than just a set of rules and regulations, see figure 3.1.

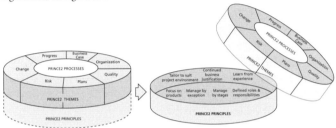

Figure 3.1 PRINCE2 is now much more based on principles (Based on OGC PRINCE2 material)

3.1 Main structural changes

- A chapter added about principles, making principles now explicit instead of implicit;
- More guidance on tailoring. This has become now a separate chapter;
- Less prescriptive. The emphasis is on working in the spirit of PRINCE2 instead of simply adhering to the regulations of the manual;
- Less bureaucratic. Sub-processes have been changed into activities. Fewer management products have been defined;
- Greater emphasis on seeking lessons;
- Improved linkage with other OGC products;
- More references to possible techniques;
- Acceptance of the reality of phased handover.

3.2   Changes to the manual

- The manual has been reduced from around 450 pages to nearer 300 pages, primarily by removing duplication;
- Components have become Themes, and have been positioned before the processes;
- There are only seven themes. Configuration Management has been integrated into the theme Change;
- The component Controls has become the theme Progress;
- The section Technique has been removed. The techniques now forming an integral part of the relevant themes;
- The number of processes has been reduced to seven; Planning is now integrated in the theme Plans;
- More guidance for Project Board members. There is a separate manual for board members entitled 'Directing Successful Projects with PRINCE2';
- The annex Risk Categories has been removed;
- The annex Health Check by Component has been replaced by a checklist by process.

3.3   Detailed changes

Themes

- **Business Case** – Post Project Review Plan is now called Benefits Review Plan and is now initially produced during Initiation and reviewed and updated at the end of each stage. Justification is based on whether the Business Case is desirable, viable or achievable. The development path of the Business Case is divided into develop, verify, maintain and confirm. The Business Case also contains an executive summary, dis-benefits and benefit tolerances.
- **Organization** – the four layers of management are now described as corporate or programme management, directing, managing

and delivering. The Change Authority role is now shown in the organization structure. The Configuration Librarian is now part of Project Support. Conforming to MSP Managing Successful Programmes, the Senior User specifies the benefits and is held to account by having to demonstrate to corporate or programme management that the forecasted benefits are realized.

- **Quality** – there is a greater focus on products. The 'path of quality' has been changed to 'quality audit trail' with two overlapping activities of quality planning and quality control. The Project Product Description is introduced, which includes the customer's quality expectations, the acceptance criteria and the project level quality tolerances. The Project Quality Plan is replaced by the Quality Management Strategy. The scope of a plan is defined as the sum total of its products.

- **Plans** – the Product Description for the final product is now known as the Project Product Description. In addition, a Product Description is now required for all identified products. The technique Product Based Planning is less prescriptive: "When presenting the product breakdown structure <u>consider</u> the use of different shapes, styles or colors for the different type of products".

- **Risks** – this whole chapter has been rewritten, so that it aligns to M_O_R™ (Management of Risk). Opportunity responses have been defined. There is recognition of the roles of Risk Owner and Risk Actionee.

- **Change** – the Daily Log is now used to record problem/concerns that can be handled informally by the Project Manager. The issue and change control procedure has been revised. The configuration management procedure has been integrated.

- **Progress** – this theme supersedes the component Control. All references to the project start-up and the controlled close have been removed.

Processes

- **Starting up a Project (SU)** – SU now includes 'Capture previous lessons'. The Project Management Team structure and role descriptions, the project approach and the Project Product Description are now part of the Project Brief. Only the Daily and Lessons Log are created in this process.
- **Directing a Project (DP)** – DP now starts after SU. The process itself remains almost the same.
- **Initiating a Project (IP)** – IP now starts with the creation of the Risk, Quality, Configuration and Communication Management Strategies. Also all the registers are created in this process. The PID is now described as the Project Initiation Documentation. The PID should state how the PRINCE2 method is being tailored.
- **Controlling a Stage (CS)** – the activities 'Capture and examine issues and risks' are now combined.
- **Managing Product Delivery (MP)** – this process remains almost the same.
- **Managing a Stage Boundary (SB)** – the activity 'Update the Risk Register' is integrated in 'update the Business Case'. The PID and the Benefits Review Plan are updated. Creating a Lessons Report and recommendations for follow-on actions may be part of this process now.
- **Closing a Project (CP)** – the Lessons Report and the follow-on actions recommendations are now part of the End Project Report. The activity 'Hand over products' is introduced.

Tailoring PRINCE2 to the project environment

This is a new chapter. Where in the past this aspect was addressed is the different chapters, this aspect is now addressed in one chapter. In addition this subject has been broadened in respect to the 2005 edition. There is distinguished embedding PRINCE2 in an organization and tailoring PRINCE2 to a project.

Special attention is given for tailoring projects in a programme environment and for tailoring PRINCE2 to the project scale, to a commercial customer/supplier environment, to multi-organization projects, to different project types and to sector differences.

Appendices

A. Product Description outlines – The number of products has been reduced from 36 to 26. Additional is the format and presentation of the individual products.

B. Governance – This appendix is new and shows how PRINCE2 addresses the governance principles published by the Association for Project Management in the UK.

C. Roles and responsibilities – The role of Change Authority has been added. The role of Project Support Office has been deleted. The role of Configuration Librarian is incorporated in the role of Project Support.

D. Product based planning example – This example is transferred from the Product based planning technique to appendix D. The Project Product Description and an example of a product breakdown structure in a format of a mind map and a simple list have been added.

E. Health check – The questions are now grouped per process in stead of per component. Special attention is given to the questions for the different activities within Direct a Project.

Further information – A short summary is given of the suite of guidance developed by the Office of Government Commerce.

Glossary – This list has been extended in respect to the 2005 Edition.

Chapter 4
Principles

The purpose of PRINCE2 is to provide a project management method that can be applied regardless of project scale, type, complexity and culture, and irrespective of the environmental factors, see figure 4.1.

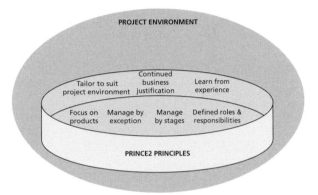

Figure 4.1 The Principles of PRINCE2® 2009 Edition (Based on OGC PRINCE2 material)

This is possible because PRINCE2 is principles-based. Principles are characterized as universal, self-validating and empowering.

4.1 Continued business justification

A requirement for each PRINCE2 project is that:
- There is a justifiable reason to start it;
- The justification may change, but should remain valid throughout the life of the project;
- The justification is documented and approved.

The justification drives the decision-making process. In PRINCE2 the justification is documented in a Business Case. Even projects that are

compulsory require justification to validate the option chosen to comply
with the compulsion.

4.2   Learn from experience

In PRINCE2 learning from experience perfects the method:
* When starting the project, previous lessons should be reviewed to see if
  these lessons could be applied;
* As the project progresses, lessons should be included in all reports and
  reviews. The goal is to seek opportunities to implement improvements
  during the life of the project;
* As the project closes, and at the intermediate stages, the project
  should pass on the lessons to the relevant corporate or programme
  organization.

It is everyone's responsibility to continuously seek lessons rather than
waiting for someone else to provide them.

4.3   Defined roles and responsibilities

A PRINCE2 project has defined and agreed roles and responsibilities,
with an organization structure that reflects the stakeholder interests of the
business, user and supplier:
* Business sponsors endorse the objectives and should ensure the business
  investment provides value for money;
* Users will use the project's products to enable them to gain the
  intended benefits;
* Suppliers will provide the resources required by the project.

Therefore all three stakeholder interests need to be represented effectively
in the project organization, at the delivery level as well as at the directing
level.

4.4   Manage by stages

A PRINCE2 project is planned, monitored and controlled on a stage-by-stage basis.

Management stages provide senior management with control at major decision points. Management stages also overcome the planning horizon by having a high level Project Plan for the total project and a detailed Stage Plan for the current stage. At the end of each stage, the next Stage Plan will be produced and the Project Plan will be updated.

PRINCE2 requires a minimum of two management stages: one initiation stage and one or more delivery stages.

4.5   Manage by exception

A PRINCE2 project has defined tolerances for each project objective to establish limits of delegating authority.

PRINCE2 enables appropriate governance by defining distinct responsibility and accountability at each level of the project by:
- Delegating authority so that tolerances are set against the objectives (time, cost, quality, scope, risk and benefit) for each level of plan;
- Establishing controls so that if those tolerances are forecast to be exceeded they are immediately referred up to the next management level for a decision on how to proceed;
- Establishing an assurance mechanism so that each management level can be confident that such controls are effective.

Management by exception provides the effective use of senior management time and reduces the time-consuming meetings that projects are normally burdened with.

4.6   Focus on products

A PRINCE2 projects focuses on the definition and delivery of products, in particular their quality requirements.

A successful project is output-oriented, not activity-oriented. An output-oriented project is one that agrees and defines the project's products including the quality requirements and acceptance criteria prior to undertaking the activities required to produce them. The set of agreed products defines the scope of a project and provides the basis for planning and control.

Without a product focus, projects are exposed to several major risks such as acceptance disputes, scope-creep, user dissatisfaction and under-estimation of acceptance activities.

4.7   Tailor to suit the project environment

PRINCE2 is tailored to suit the project's environment, size, complexity, importance, capability and risk:
- Ensure the project management method relates to the project environment such as industry-specific models, corporate standards, organizational maturity and culture;
- Ensure that the project controls are based on the project's factors such as scale, complexity, importance, capability and risks.

Tailoring requires an active decision on how the method will be applied. To ensure that all people involved understand how the method is being tailored, it should be stated in the PID how the method is being tailored for that particular project.

Chapter 5
Introduction to PRINCE2 Themes

The PRINCE2 themes describe the aspects of project management that must be addressed continually and integrally throughout the project, see figure 5.1.

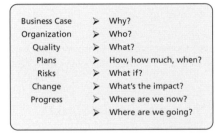

Business Case	➤ Why?
Organization	➤ Who?
Quality	➤ What?
Plans	➤ How, how much, when?
Risks	➤ What if?
Change	➤ What's the impact?
Progress	➤ Where are we now?
	➤ Where are we going?

Figure 5.1 The PRINCE2 Themes (Based on OGC PRINCE2 material)

Business Case – describes how the idea is developed into a viable investment proposition for the organization and how project management maintains the focus on the organization's objectives throughout the project.

Organization – describes the roles and responsibilities in the temporary project organization that are required to manage the project effectively.

Quality – describes how the original outline is developed into the quality criteria and how project management ensures that these criteria are subsequently delivered.

Plans – describes the steps required to develop plans and suggests the Product Based Planning technique to be applied.

Risks – describes how project management manages the uncertainties in plans and in the wider project environment.

Change – describes how project management assesses and acts upon issues which have a potential impact on any of the baseline aspects of the project. Issues may be unanticipated problems or concerns, requests for change, or instances of quality failure.

Progress – addresses the ongoing viability of the plans. This then explains the decision-making process for approving plans, the monitoring of the actual performance, the corrective actions to be taken and the escalation process if the performance is forecast to exceed the agreed tolerances.

All seven themes must be applied throughout the project, but should be tailored according to the project context.

Chapter 6
Business Case

6.1 Purpose

The purpose of the Business Case theme is to establish mechanisms by which to judge whether the project is and remains desirable, viable and achievable, as a means to support the decision making in relation to its investment.

A project must have continued business justification. The Business Case is owned by the Executive. In some projects there is a pre-defined Business Case, in which case it will be refined during initiation.

6.2 Business Case defined

In PRINCE2 the Business Case is defined as follows:
- **Output** – any of the project's specialist products (whether tangible or intangible);
- **Outcome** – the result of the change derived from using these outputs;
- **Benefit** – the measurable improvement resulting from an outcome that is perceived as an achievement by a stakeholder.

The nature of the project will determine the objectives that will be used to verify the desirability of the project and later to confirm that the project actually met those objectives. Those objectives may be measured differently depending on the type of project, for example:
- Compulsory project;
- Not-for profit project;
- Evolving project;
- Customer/supplier project;
- Multi-organization project.

Some of these projects may be measured principally on return on investment, but others may be measured on non-financial benefits. Regardless of the type of benefits, for each investment the question remains, are the anticipated benefits more desirable, viable and achievable than the other options available?

6.3   PRINCE2 approach to Business Case

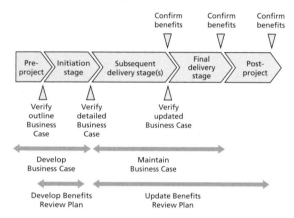

Figure 6.1 The development path of the Business Case (Source: Managing Successful Projects with PRINCE2, produced by OGC)

The Business Case is **developed** at the beginning of the project (or before) and **maintained** throughout the life of the project, being formally **verified** by the Project Board at each key decision point, such as end stage assessments, so that it can be **confirmed** throughout the period that the expected benefits are being accrued, see figure 6.1.

Alongside the Business Case, the Benefits Review Plan is developed, maintained and verified. The Business Review Plan is the basis upon which to review and measure the benefits.

6.3.1. Developing the Business Case

The Executive owns the Business Case. However the development of the Business Case may be delegated to a business analyst or even to the Project Manager. The Project Board should consider using Project Assurance to assist with the development of the Business Case.

The outline Business Case is developed in the process Starting up a Project and is integrated in the Project Brief. The outline Business Case may be derived from the project mandate. In the process Initiating a Project, the full Business Case will be developed.

It is worth noting that the supplier can have its own Business Case, particularly if the supplier is an external party. However the Business Case in a project is usually referred to as the Business Case of the customer.

6.3.2. Verifying and maintaining the Business Case

The Business Case is verified and maintained as follows:
- At the end of Starting up a Project by the Project Board to authorize the project initiation;
- At the end of Initiating a Project by the Project Board to authorize the project;
- As part of any impact assessment by the Project Manager;
- As part of the Exception Plan by the Project Board to authorize the revised stage and continuation of the project;
- At the end of each stage by the Project Manager;
- At the end of each stage by the Project Board to authorize the next stage and the continuation of the project;
- During the final stage by the Project Manager;
- At the closure of the project by the Project Board to verify an accurate basis for the benefits review to be carried out;
- As part of the benefits review to determine the success of the project outcomes in realizing their benefits.

It is the responsibility of the Executive to assure the project's stakeholders that the project remains desirable, viable and achievable at all times.

6.3.3. Confirming the benefits
The approach to confirm the benefits is to:
* Identify the benefits;
* Select objective measures that reliably prove the benefits;
* Collect the baseline measures;
* Decide how, when and by whom the benefits measures will be collected.

The Senior User(s) specifies the benefits and is held to account by having to demonstrate to corporate or programme management that the forecast benefits are in fact being realized.

The Benefits Review Plan is first created in the initiation stage and updated during the subsequent stage boundaries, and is finally updated at Closing a Project by the Project Manager.

6.4   The contents of a Business Case

The Business Case should include the following:
* **Executive summary;**
* **Reasons:** why this project is required and how the project will support the corporate strategies and objectives;
* **Business options**: with at least the options: do nothing, do the minimum and do something. All other options should be compared with the do nothing option;
* **Expected benefits**: whether financial or non-financial. All benefits should be aligned to corporate objectives and strategies, mapped from the outputs provided by the project, quantified, measurable and owned. Set a benefit tolerance for each benefit;

- **Expected dis-benefits**: an outcome perceived as negative by one or more stakeholders;
- **Timescale**: the period during which the project costs will be incurred and the period upon which the cost/benefits analysis will be based;
- **Costs**: derived from the Project Plan together with the assumptions upon which they are based, inclusive the ongoing operations and maintenance costs and their funding arrangements;
- **Investment appraisal**: assessment of the development, operational and maintenance costs against the value of the benefits over a period of time;
- **Major risks**: summary of the aggregated risks (risk profile) and a highlight of the major risks.

6.5 Responsibilities of the Business Case theme

For the responsibilities relevant to the Business Case theme, see table 6.1:

Corporate / programme management	Project Manager (PM)
• Provide mandate and define any standards for development of the Business Case (BC) • Hold Senior User to account for realizing the benefits • Accountable for Benefits Review Plan (post-project) **Executive** • Owns Business Case for duration of project • Approves Benefits Review Plan • Ensure alignment of project with business strategies • Secure funding **Senior User** • Specify the benefits upon which the BC is approved • Ensure the desired project outcome is specified • Ensure that project produces products which deliver the desired outcomes • Ensure the expected benefits are realized • Provide actual versus forecast benefits statement at benefits reviews **Senior Supplier** • Approve supplier's Business Case (if any) • Confirm that the products required can be delivered within expected costs and time	• Prepare the BC on behalf of the Executive • Conduct impact analyses on issues and risks that may affect project's viability • Assess and update the BC at the end of each management stage • Assess and report on project performance at project closure **Project Assurance** • Assist in development of the BC • Ensure viability of the BC is constantly reassessed • Monitor changes to the Project Plan to identify any impact on the BC • Verify and monitor BC against issues and progress • Review impact assessments on Project Plan and BC • Monitor project finance on behalf of the customer • Ensure project stays aligned with corporate or programme strategy • Verify and monitor Benefits Review Plan for alignment to corporate or programme management **Project Support** • Keep the Business Case under configuration • Advice PM about changes that may affect the Business Case

Table 6.1 Roles and responsibilities of the Business Case theme (Based on OGC PRINCE2 material)

Chapter 7
Organization

7.1 Purpose

The purpose of the Organization theme is to define and establish the project's structure of accountability and responsibilities.

PRINCE2 is based on a customer/supplier environment. It assumes that there is a customer who will specify the desired result and probably pay for the project, and a supplier who will provide the resources and skills to deliver that result. Suppliers and customers can be part of the same organization. They can also be part of different organizations. Within the customer we can again recognize users and business representatives.

A successful project management team should:
- Have business, user and supplier representation;
- Ensure appropriate governance by defining responsibilities for directing, managing and delivering the project;
- Have an effective strategy to engage the stakeholders;
- Have reviews of the project roles to ensure the continuous effectiveness of the team.

7.2 Organization defined

PRINCE2 states that a project always has three primary categories of stakeholders and that their interests must be satisfied in the project if the project is to be successful. In order to realize this it is necessary to have business, user and supplier representation at the management level of the project, see figure 7.1.

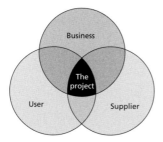

Figure 7.1 The three project interests (Source: Managing Successful Projects with PRINCE2, produced by OGC)

The business – are those who will need to have a business need in order to justify the investment in the project. The project should provide value for money for them.

The users – are those who will use the project's output, will operate, maintain or support the output, or will be affected by the output.

The suppliers – are those who will provide the necessary resources and skills and deliver the project's product.

7.3 Levels of organization

Within a project we can recognize three levels of organization:

- Directing;
- Managing;
- Delivering.

In small projects managing and delivering will sometimes be combined. These three groups are represented in the project management team.

The project management structure has four layers; the above three layers together with corporate or programme management, see figure 7.2.

Figure 7.2 Levels of management (Source: Managing Successful Projects with PRINCE2, produced by OGC)

Corporate or programme management – this level sits outside the project management team, but is responsible for commissioning the project and giving overall direction within the corporate or programme strategy. It is accountable for realizing the benefits as they have been agreed that these should result from the project's output.

Directing – the Project Board is responsible for the overall direction of the project and management of the project within the constraints set out by corporate or programme management.

Managing – the Project Manager is responsible for the day-to-day management of the projects within the constraints set out by the Project Board.

Delivering – the Team Manager is responsible for the daily management of the individual Work Packages and for the delivery of the project output within the defined objectives.

The project organization consists of the first three layers of management and team members. The team members are responsible for the actual realization of the project's products.

7.4   Project management team

The project management team is the temporary structure set up to manage the project. In addition to the Project Board, Project Manager and Team Manager(s) it also consists of Project Assurance, Change Authority and Project Support, see figure 7.3.

Project Board – the highest management level of the project. The board contains the roles of Executive, Senior User and Senior Supplier. The responsibilities of the Project Board are:

- Being accountable for the success of the project;
- Providing unified direction and guidance;
- Delegating effectively to the Project Manager;
- Facilitating the integration of the functional units;
- Providing funding and the resources required;
- Ensuring effective decision making;
- Ensuring effective communication within the project team and with external stakeholders.

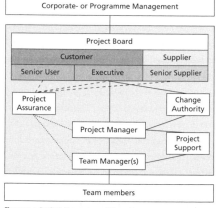

Figure 7.3 Project Management Team (Source: Managing Successful Projects with PRINCE2, produced by OGC)

A good Project Board displays authority, credibility, ability to delegate and availability.

Executive – located within the Project Board, and is ultimately accountable for the success of the project and is the key decision maker. In this respect the Project Board is not a democratic entity, but a management platform for decision making. The Executive is responsible for the continuous viability of the project from the customer point of view. There should be only one Executive.

Senior User – represents the interests of the users on the Project Board. Within this the Senior User is responsible for specifying the needs of the users, reviewing the project's products from the users' point of view, making available the necessary user resources and communicating about the project with other user representatives. The Senior User is also responsible for specifying the benefits and is held to account by having to demonstrate to corporate or programme management that the forecasted benefits are in fact being realized. This role can be fulfilled by more than one person.

Senior Supplier – represents the interests of the suppliers on the Project Board. The Senior Supplier is accountable for the (quality of the) products delivered by the suppliers. Within this he is responsible for providing the suppliers' resources and skills, and ensuring that the proposals for design and realization are feasible and realistic. This role can be fulfilled by more than one person.

Project Assurance – is the derivative responsibility of the Project Board. Project Assurance monitors all aspects of the project's performance and products independently from the Project Manager, to release the board members from their supervision responsibilities. Project Assurance is aligned to the business, user and supplier areas of interest.

The Project Board needs to represent all interested parties. Therefore several Senior Users and Suppliers could be appointed. However, to avoid an unworkable board, it is good practice to appoint separate user and supplier groups who will be represented on the board by a limited number of senior staff, see figure 7.4.

Change Authority – is also a delegated responsibility of the Project Board. The Change Authority is the person or group to which the Project Board delegates (partially) the responsibility for the consideration of requests for change and off-specifications.

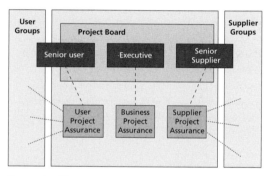

Figure 7.4 Possible structure using user and supplier groups (based on OGC PRINCE2 material)

Project Manager – is responsible for the day-to-day management of the project on behalf of the Project Board. Within this the Project Manager is responsible for the planning of the works, authorizing the Work Packages, monitoring the progress and taking corrective actions if necessary. If it is forecast that agreed tolerances will be exceeded, he has to escalate this to the Project Board for a decision. The Project Manager should align with Project Assurance. The role of Project Manager should not be shared.

Team Manager – is responsible for ensuring the production of those products allocated to him by the Project Manager. The Team Manager reports to, and takes directions from, the Project Manager. The responsibility of the Team Manager to the Project Manager is a delegated responsibility from the Senior Supplier towards the Executive. In many projects there is more than one Team Manager.

Project Support – is the derivative responsibility of the Project Manager. Project Support normally provides administrative services as well as specialist functions such as planning and budgetary control. Project Support is typically responsible for administering configuration services and maintaining Risk, Issue and Quality Registers.

7.5   Communication Management Strategy

The Communication Management Strategy contains a description of the means and frequency of communication to internal and external stakeholders of the project. The strategy is developed in the process Initiating a Project and is updated at the stage boundaries.

The Project Manager is responsible for documenting and maintaining the strategy. The Executive is accountable for the effectiveness of the strategy. The actual communication activities are built into the appropriate plans and are monitored from there by the Project Manager.

Chapter 8
Quality

8.1 Purpose

The purpose of the Quality theme is to define and implement the means by which the project will create and verify products that are fit for purpose.

The quality theme defines the PRINCE2 approach to ensure that the project's products meet business expectations and that the desired benefits will be subsequently achieved.

The product focus is central to the PRINCE2 approach to quality, and is applicable for the specialist products as well for the management products of the project. Capturing and acting upon the lessons learnt contributes to the quality approach, as it is a means by which continuous improvement can be achieved.

8.2 Quality definitions

Quality is, in general, defined as the totality of the features and characteristics of a product that impact upon its ability to meet a stated need, be it self-evident or obligatory.

The scope of a plan is the sum of its products and the respective activities required to realize them. Within PRINCE2 the scope of a plan is limited to the sum of its products and is defined by its product breakdown structure and its associated Product Descriptions.

8.3   Quality management

Quality management is defined as the coordinated activities required to direct and control an organization with regard to quality. A quality management system (QMS) is the complete set of quality standards, procedures and responsibilities for a site or organization.

In the project context, sites and organizations should be interpreted as the (semi-)permanent organizations sponsoring the project work, i.e. they are external to the project's temporary organization. Only a huge project may have a QMS by itself.

The quality approach in a project is derived from the QMSs of the respective customer and supplier organizations.

Quality planning – is the aspect of quality management aimed at defining the quality objectives and the specification of the necessary operational processes, together with the means by which to meet these quality objectives. Quality planning is about defining the products required, with their respective quality criteria and quality methods, and the quality responsibilities of those involved.

Quality control – is the aspect of quality management aimed at ensuring compliance with the quality criteria of products. Quality control focuses on the operational techniques and activities used to fulfill the quality requirements (e.g. a quality review, see table 8.1) or to identify ways of eliminating causes of unsatisfactory performance (e.g. introducing process improvements as a result of lessons learned).

Quality assurance – is the aspect of quality management aimed at providing confidence that customer expectations will be met. Quality assurance is a process-driven approach best known through the Deming

Quality Review Technique	
An involved partnership designed to assess conformity of a product against a set of quality criteria by means of a review procedure	
Objectives	**Team roles**
• To assess conformity against criteria	• Chair, responsible for overall conduct of the review
• To promote wider acceptance of the product	• Presenter, to represent the producers of the product
• To provide confirmation that the product is ready for approval	• Reviewer(s) to review the product and confirm corrections and/or improvements
• To baseline the product for change control purpose	• Administrator to provide administrative support and record the actions and results

Table 8.1 Quality review technique (Based on OGC PRINCE2 material)

Cycle, developed by Dr. W. Edwards Deming. *Plan*, *Do*, *Check*, and *Act*. Within PRINCE2 quality assurance is defined as a responsibility of the corporate or programme management only, and therefore outside the scope of a project and, thus, also outside the scope of PRINCE2. Quality assurance responsibilities within the project are considered to be part of the broader responsibility of project assurance within the project, see table 8.2.

Project Assurance	Quality Assurance
Assurance to the project's stakeholders that the project is being conducted appropriately and properly and complies with the plans and standards agreed	Assurance to the corporate or programme management that the project is conducted appropriately and properly and complies with the relevant corporate or programme standards and policies
Must be independent of the Project Manager and project team	Must be independent of the project management team
Responsibility of the Project Board	Responsibility of the corporate or programme organization
Corporate or programme quality assurance function can be used by the Project Board as part of the Project Assurance regime (e.g. to conduct quality audits)	Proper Project Assurance can provide confidence that the relevant corporate or programme standards and policies are met.

Table 8.2 Relationship between Project and Quality Assurance within PRINCE2 (Based on OGC PRINCE2 material)

8.4   PRINCE2 approach to quality

The PRINCE2 approach to quality leads to systematic activities in terms
of the following, see figure 8.1.

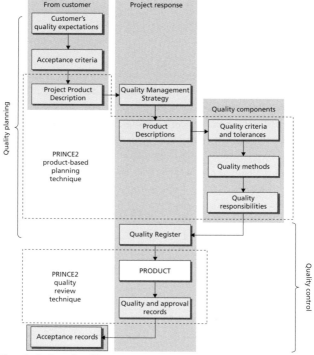

Figure 8.1 Quality audit trail (Source: Managing Successful Projects with PRINCE2, produced by OGC)

Quality planning consists of developing the Quality Management Strategy and defining the customer's quality expectations and acceptance criteria, which are documented in the Project Product Description.

Quality control consists of the planning and control of the operational techniques and activities to comply with the product's quality criteria, which are documented in the Quality Register and the quality, approval and acceptance records.

Customer quality expectations describe the quality expected from the project's product. Acceptance criteria are the criteria that the project's product must meet before the customer will accept it. Together with project-level quality tolerances and acceptance method and responsibilities, these are both captured in the Project Product Description.

The Quality Management Strategy describes the quality techniques and standards to be applied, and the various responsibilities for achieving the required quality levels.

The Product Description describes what is needed to develop the product, the quality criteria the product must meet, how and by whom the quality criteria must be reviewed and who is responsible for approving the product.

The Quality Register records all quality management activities that are planned and/or have taken place, the quality responsibilities, the quality results and the references to the respective quality records.

8.5   Responsibilities of the Quality theme

For the responsibilities relevant to the Quality theme, see table 8.3.

Corporate / programme management	Project Manager (PM)
• Approve application of corporate/ programme Quality Management Strategy (QMS) • Bring into action Quality Assurance	• Document CQE and AC • Prepare Project Product Description • Prepare Quality Mgt Strategy • Prepare and maintain PDs • Ensure TM's implement agreed quality control measures
Executive	
• Approve Project Product Description • Approve Quality Mgt Strategy • Confirm acceptance of project product	**Team Manager (TM)** • Implement agreed quality control measures • Produce products consistent with PD's • Manage quality controls for Work Package's products • Assemble quality records • Advise PM about product quality status
Senior User	
• customer quality expectations (cqe) • acceptance criteria (ac) • Approve Project Product Description • Approve Quality Mgt Strategy • Approve Product Descriptions (PD) for (key) products • Provide user resources for quality activities • Communicate with user stakeholders • Provide project product acceptance	**Project Assurance** • Advise Project Board and PM on project's Quality Mgt Strategy • Assist PB and PM in reviewing PDs • Advise PM on suitable quality reviewers • Assure PB on implementing strategies
Senior Supplier	**Project Support**
• Approve Project Product Description • Approve Quality Mgt Strategy • Approve quality methods, techniques & tools • Approve PD for key specialist products • Provide supplier resources for quality activities • Communicate with supplier stakeholders	• Provide administrative support of quality controls • Maintain Quality Register & quality records • Assist with project quality processes

Table 8.3 Roles and responsibilities of the Quality theme (Based on OGC PRINCE2 material)

Chapter 9
Plans

9.1 Purpose

The purpose of the Plans theme is to facilitate realization, communications and control by defining the means through which the products will be delivered. The Plans theme provides a framework to design, develop and maintain the project's plans.

9.2 Plans defined

A plan is a document, describing *how, when* and by *whom* a specific target or set of targets is to be achieved. Planning is the act or process of making and maintaining a plan.

PRINCE2 recommends three levels of plans to reflect the needs of the different levels of management involved in the project:
- Project Plan;
- Stage Plan;
- Team Plan.

In addition PRINCE2 recognizes the Exception Plan, which is prepared in order to show the actions required to recover from the effect of a tolerance deviation. Each plan is derived from the parent plan. There is an initiation Stage Plan and there are delivery Stage Plans, see figure 9.1.

Project Plan – is used by the Project Board as a baseline against which to monitor a project's progress stage-by-stage. The Project Plan should align with the corporate or programme plan. The Project Plan identifies the milestones and management stages and provides the Business Case with planned project costs and timescales. The Project Plan is created in the initiation stage and will be updated at the end of each management stage. The Project Plan is developed and maintained by the Project Manager and approved by the Project Board.

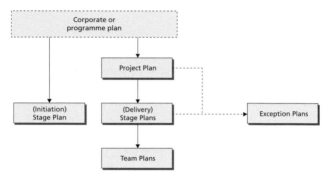

Figure 9.1 PRINCE2 planning levels (Source: Managing Successful Projects with PRINCE2, produced by OGC)

Stage Plan – is required for each management stage. In composition the Stage Plan is similar to the Project Plan. The Stage Plan is the basis for the day-to-day control by the Project Manager. The next Stage Plan is produced near the end of the current management stage. For projects with only one delivery stage, the delivery Stage Plan can be incorporated in the Project Plan. The Stage Plan is developed and maintained by the Project Manager and is approved by the Project Board.

Team Plan – is optional. If required it is created during the development of the parent Stage Plan, or when accepting a Work Package. The Team Plan is produced or amended by a Team Manager and is approved by the Project Manager. PRINCE2 does not describe the format or composition of a Team Plan. With external suppliers, a Team Plan often contains summary information intended only to exercise control. The Senior Supplier is accountable for the Team Plan.

Exception Plan – will replace the plan in which deviations have occurred that are outside tolerance limits and will, after approval, become the new baselined Project Plan or Stage Plan. The format of the Exception Plan is the same as the plan it replaces. The Exception Plan covers the remaining period of the plan it replaces and will be approved by the next higher level of management.

If a Work Package is in exception, the Team Manager raises the issue to the Project Manager. If the exception can be resolved within the stage tolerances, the Project Manager will take corrective actions by updating the Work Package and instructing the Team Manager accordingly. It is then the Team Manager's responsibility to renew/update the Team Plan to incorporate the actions required to recover from the effect of the tolerance deviation.

9.3 PRINCE2 approach to plans

The PRINCE2 approach to plans is that firstly the products required are identified, prior to the activities, dependencies and resources required being identified. This is known as Product-based Planning, see figure 9.2.

Before plans can be developed, decisions have to be made about the presentation and lay-out of the plans, the planning tools, estimating methods, levels of plans and monitoring methods to be used for the project. Any specific variations from the corporate or programme standards should be highlighted

The defining and analyzing of the products can be done best through the use of a product–based planning technique.

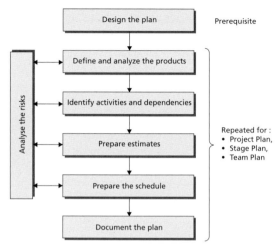

Figure 9.2 PRINCE2 approach to plans (Source: Managing Successful Projects with PRINCE2, produced by OGC)

After the products have been identified and specified, the activities and dependencies between the activities should be identified in order to enable the respective products to be produced. Based on the activities and dependencies, estimates can be made and a time schedule can be established. In parallel the identified risks should be analyzed. Risk activities should be incorporated. Finally, the documents will be assembled and the plan documented.

9.4   Product-based planning technique

The product-based planning technique comprises four steps, as shown in figure 9.3.

Project Product Description – the project product is the ultimate end result to be delivered by the project. The Project Product Description

describes the major product(s) to be delivered by the project, the source
products from which the product is derived, the development skills needed,
the customer quality expectations and acceptance criteria, the project
tolerances and the acceptance methods and responsibilities.

The Senior User is responsible for specifying the project product. In
practice the Project Product Description is written by Project Manager in
consultation with the Executive and Senior User.

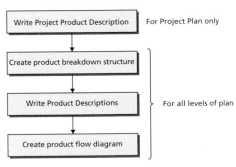

Figure 9.3 Product-based planning technique (Source: Managing Successful Projects with PRINCE2,
produced by OGC)

Product breakdown structure (pbs) – the project product is broken down
until an appropriate level of detail for the plan is achieved. A lower-level
product can be a component of only one higher-level product. A pbs
should not contain any loops. A pbs is required for each separate stage.
Groupings and external products should preferably be distinguished in
form and/or color, where external products are products that already exist,
or are created or updated outside the scope of the project.

Each external product should have a corresponding entry in the Risk
Register. Even external products may require a Product Description.
Furthermore, consideration may be given to including different states of a

product when the responsibility for each state differs. A PBS can be used to create a work breakdown structure

Product Description – is required for all identified products. A Product Description is written immediately after the product has been identified and will be frozen after the respective Stage Plan is approved. Although the Project or Team Manager is responsible for writing the Product Descriptions, it is wise to involve user representatives and material experts. A detailed requirement specification can be used as a substitute. For small projects the Project Product Description may be sufficient.

Product flow diagram (pfd) – is required to define the sequence in which the products will be developed and any dependencies between them. The pfd can be created in parallel with pbs. A pfd flows in one direction only and should not contain any loops. External products should be included, though groupings should not.

All products, with the exception of external products and the start and end product, should have one or more input and output relations. It is advisable to start the pfd from one single product or the PID. The end product is the project product

Figure 9.4 Product Breakdown Structure of PRINCE2 Management Products (Based on OGC PRINCE2 material)

It is advisable to include the management products in the planning. PRINCE2 identifies baseline products, records and reports, see figure 9.4. In the product flow diagram the planned event-driven management products should be included.

9.5 Responsibilities of the Plans theme

For the responsibilities relevant to the Plans theme, see table 9.1.

Corporate / programme management	Project Manager (PM)
Corporate / programme management • Provide corporate/ programme planning standards • Define project tolerances in mandate • Approve project Exception Plans **Executive** • Approve Project Plan • Define stage tolerances • Approve Stage and Exception Plans • Commit business resources to Stage Plans **Senior User** • Ensure Project and Stage Plans remain consistent from user perspective • Commit user resources to Stage Plans **Senior Supplier** • Ensure Project and Stage Plans remain consistent from supplier perspective • Commit supplier resources to Stage Plans	**Project Manager (PM)** • Develop Project and Stage Plans • Designs management and technical stages • Instruct corrective actions when Work Package tolerances are forecasted to exceed • Prepare stage and project Exception Reports **Team Manager (TM)** • Create and update Team Plans • Prepare schedules for each Work Package • Escalate to PM when Work Package tolerances are forecasted to exceed **Project Assurance** • Monitor changes to the Project Plan on impact to the Business Case • Monitor stage and project progress against agreed tolerances **Project Support** • Assist with development plans • Contribute with specialist expertise • Baseline and store plans

Table 9.1 Roles and responsibilities of the Plans theme (Based on OGC PRINCE2 material)

Chapter 10
Risks

10.1 Purpose

The purpose of the Risk theme is to identify, assess and control uncertainty and, as a result, improve the ability of the project to succeed.

Risk management should be systematic, focused on the proactive identification, assessment and control of risks. Effective risk management is a prerequisite of the continued business justification principle.

10.2 Risk defined

It is important to distinguish between risks and issues:
- **Issue** – a relevant event that has occurred and was not planned, and that requires management attention;
- **Risk** – an uncertain event or set of events that, <u>if it occurs</u>, will have an effect on the achievement of the objectives.

Risks can be distinguished in terms of threats and opportunities:
- **Threat** – an uncertain event that could have a <u>negative</u> impact on objectives;
- **Opportunity** – an uncertain event that could have a <u>positive</u> impact on objectives.

A risk can contain threats as well as opportunities at the same time. Therefore threats and opportunities should both be managed as risks.

Risk management is the systematic application of procedures to the tasks of identifying and assessing risk, and then planning and implementing risk responses. For effective risk management, risks should be properly identified, assessed and controlled.

PRINCE2 recommends that every project should have its own Risk Management Strategy and a Risk Register.

10.3 Risk Management Strategy

This strategy should be separated from the corporate or programme risk management strategy and policies.

The Risk Management Strategy describes how risk management will be embedded in the project management activities. A key decision that needs to be recorded in the strategy is the Project Board's attitude towards risks, which in turn dictates the level of risk that is considered acceptable, and this is reflected in the risk tolerances.

Furthermore, the Risk Management Strategy describes levels of probability, impact and proximity, and risk, together with the risk response categories, early warning indicators and the risk budget.

10.4 Risk Register

The purpose of the Risk Register is to capture and maintain the information on all the identified risks related to the project. Project Support will typically maintain the Risk Register on behalf of the Project Manager. The Risk Management Strategy will describe the procedure for registering risks and maintaining the Risk Register.

10.5 Risk management procedures

PRINCE2 recommends a risk management procedure comprising the
following five steps, see figure. 10.1.

Fig. 10.1 Risk management procedure (Source: Managing Successful Projects with PRINCE2, produced by OGC)

Identify:
* Identify context – obtain information about the project in order to
  understand the specific objectives of the project and formulate the Risk
  Management Strategy;
* Identify risks – capture the individual risks that may impact upon the
  project's objectives. Provide a clear and unambiguous expression of each
  risk by describing its cause, the risk itself and the effect of the risk on
  the project's objectives, see figure 10.2.

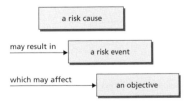

Figure 10.2 Risk cause, event and effect (Source: Managing Successful Projects with PRINCE2, produced by OGC)

Prepare early warning indicators to monitor critical aspects of the project. Provide information on the potential sources of risks. Assess the respective risk categories. Understand the stakeholders' view of the specific risks captured. Assign temporary risk owners. Record the risks and their features in the Risk Register.

Project risks are risks which have an impact on the project's objectives and via that on the business. Business risks are risks which have a direct effect on the performance of the business itself.

Assess

- Estimate – estimate the probability, impact and proximity, and the risk category of the individual risks. Often the individual risk will be presented in a summary risk profile, see figure 10.3. Confirm the assignment of the individual risk owners;

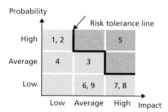

Figure 10.3 Example of summary risk profile (Based on OGC PRINCE2 material)

- Evaluate – assess the net effect of all the individual risks on a project when aggregated together. This will enable an assessment of whether the aggregated risks are within the defined risk tolerances and if the project has a continued business justification. Aggregated risks are often expressed in an expected monetary value, see table 10.1, which in turn frequently forms the basis for the assignment of the risk budget.

Risk	Probability	Impact	Expected value
A	30%	€ 50.000	€ 15.000
B	60%	€ 25.000	€ 15.000
C	20%	€ 100.000	€ 20.000
Total	Expected monetary value		€ 50.000

Table 10.1 Example of expected monetary value (Based on OGC PRINCE2 material)

Plan

• Response options – identify and evaluate the different response options and their possible consequences for the project, see figure 10.4.

Effect	Threat Responses	Opportunity Responses
High	Avoid	Exploit
↑	Reduce / Fallback / Transfer	Enhance
↓	Share	
Low	Accept	Reject

Figure 10.4 Threats and opportunities responses (Based on OGC PRINCE2 material)

- *Avoid*: make sure the threat does not exist any more;
- *Reduce*: proactive action to reduce the probability or impact;
- *Fallback*: put in place a fallback plan (reduction of impact);
- *Transfer*: make a third party responsible (e.g. insurance);
- *Share*: choose a pain-gain formula;
- *Accept:* a deliberate decision to monitor only;
- *Exploit*: make sure the opportunity will happen;
- *Enhance*: actions to increase probability or profit;
- *Reject:* a deliberate decision not to take action.

- Build the individual responses into the appropriate plans after approval of the responses and plans by the responsible authorities.

Implement
- Ensure that the role and responsibilities of the risk owners and risk actionees have been assigned, accepted and understood properly;
- Ensure that the planned risk responses are actioned;
- Monitor the effectiveness of the risk responses;
- Take corrective actions where it is evident that responses do not match the expectations.

A risk owner is the individual who is responsible for the management, monitoring and control of all aspects of a particular risk, including the risk responses. The risk owner reports on the risk to the Project Manager.

A risk actionee is the individual who is assigned to carry out a specific risk response. The risk actionee reports on the risk response to the risk owner.

Communicate
- Communicate the status of the risks within the project management team and confirm the Communication Management Strategy to the external stakeholders. Risks should be an item of concern in every report and meeting.

10.6 Responsibilities of the Risk theme

For the responsibilities that are relevant to the Risk theme, see table 10.2.

Corporate / programme management
- Provide risk management policy
- Provide risk management process guide

Executive
- Approve Risk Management Strategy
- Responsible for business risks
- Escalate risk to corporate or programme management

Project Board
- Inform PM about external risks
- Take decision on risks

Senior User
- Ensure user aspects of risks are managed

Senior Supplier
- Ensure supplier aspects of risks are managed

Project Manager (PM)
- Create Risk Management Strategy
- Create and maintain Risk Register
- Responsible for management of risks

Team Manager (TM)
- Participate in identifying, assessing and controlling risks

Project Assurance
- Review risk management practices
- Ensure alignment with strategy

Project Support
- Assist PM in maintaining Risk Register

Risk owner
- Management of individual risk

Risk actionee
- Carry out risk response action

Table 10.2 Roles and responsibilities of the Risks theme (Based on OGC PRINCE2 material)

Chapter 11
Change

11.1   Purpose

The purpose of the Change theme is to identify, assess and control any potential and approved issues and changes to the baseline.

The purpose of Issue and Change Control is not to prevent changes. It is to ensure that every issue and change is agreed by the relevant authority before it takes place. Changes have a direct impact on Product Descriptions.

A prerequisite of effective change control is the establishment of an appropriate Configuration Management system, which records baselines for the project's product.

11.2   Change defined

Issue and Change Control (CC) is the procedure which ensures that all changes that may effect the project's objectives are identified, assessed, and either approved, rejected of deferred

An issue is a relevant but unplanned event that has happened, and requires management action. A change is the alteration of a baseline, where the baseline is a reference level against which an entity is monitored and controlled. By definition, therefore, a change is a sub-set of an issue.

PRINCE2 recognizes three types of issues:
- Request for change – a proposal for a change of a baseline;
- Off-specification – something that should be provided by the project, but currently is not, or is forecast not to be;
- Problem/concern – any other issue that the Project Manager needs to resolve or escalate.

Configuration Management (CM) is the technical and administrative activity concerned with the creation, maintenance and controlled change of a Configuration Item.

Configuration Item (CI) is an entity that is subject to Configuration Management. The entity may be a component of a product, or a set of products in a release.

11.3 PRINCE2 approach to Change

The project's controls for issues and changes are defined and established in the initiation stage, see chapter 13, and then reviewed and updated towards the end of each management stage, where this is not the end of the project.

Management products to establish and maintain a project's controls for issues and changes are:
- Configuration Management Strategy;
- Configuration Item Records;
- Product Status Account;
- Daily Log;
- Issue Register;
- Issue Report.

The **Configuration Management Strategy** defines the way issues should be handled. It should define:

- The Configuration Management procedure;
- Issue and Change Control procedure;
- Records to be kept, tools and techniques to be used;
- How performances will be reported;
- Timing of CC and CM activities;
- Roles and responsibilities in respect to CC and CM;
- Scales for priority and severity.

A widely recognized scale for priority and severity is, for instance, MoSCoW: Must have – Should have – Could have – Won't have for now.

Configuration Item Records is a set of records that describes the features, such as status and version, of each CI and includes details of important relationships between these CIs. Configuration Items Records are usually stored in a Configuration Management Database (CMDB).

A **Product Status Account** provides information about the status of CIs. It is particularly useful if the Project Manager wishes to confirm the version and status of the CIs, e.g. at the end of a management stage, at the end of the project, or as part of examining issues and risks.

The **Daily Log** is the project diary for the Project Manager. In this context it is used to record problems/concerns that can be handled informally by the Project Manager.

The issues which should be managed formally are captured in the **Issue Register**. The Issue Register should be maintained and monitored by the Project Manager on a regular basis.

For each issue captured in the Issue Register, an **Issue Report** should be created. The Issue Reports should be maintained and monitored in parallel with the Issue Register. An Issue Report contains all the relevant information in relation to the respective issue.

11.4 Configuration Management procedure

Configuration Management normally comprises five steps:

- **Planning:** decide which products will be managed under formal Configuration Management, at what level in the product breakdown individual CIs will be captured and managed, which attributes of the CIs will be recorded, and will this level of management will be achieved and maintained;
- **Identification**: identify, specify and record all of the defined CIs and store all Configuration Item Records in a CMDB;
- **Control**: make sure that all relevant information is stored and can be retrieved, update CIs only after the changes have been authorized, archive old baseline versions, ensure safety and security of the CIs, and distribute copies if authorized. 'Nothing moves or changes without authorization';
- **Status accounting**: report all current and historical data concerning the CIs in a Project Status Account;
- **Verification and audit**: compare the actual status of all CIs against the Configuration Items Records as documented in the Project Status Account. Audit the performance of the configuration procedure.

11.5 Issue and change control procedure

Issue and change control also normally comprises five steps, see figure 11.1.

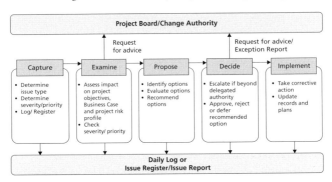

Figure 11.1 Issue and change control procedure (Source: Managing Successful Projects with PRINCE2, produced by OGC)

- **Capture**: determine if an issue can be handled informally or not. Determine the type, severity and priority of the issue. Log the issues which should be handled formally in the Issue Register. Create an Issue Report to capture what is already known about the issue;
- **Examine**: assess the impact on project objectives, project risk profile and the Business Case from business, user and supplier perspectives. Check the severity and priority and, if required, request advice;
- **Propose**: identify and evaluate options, including the cost-benefit of each option in relation to the interests of the project and its stakeholders;
- **Decide**: decide upon the corrective actions to be taken. Forward requests for change to the respective change authority. Escalate an Exception Report if issues are forecast to exceed agreed tolerances.

The Project Board can:
- Approve the change or accept the off-specification without corrective actions (concession);
- Reject the change or instruct the off-specification to be resolved;
- Defer the decision to a later date;
- Request more information;
- Provide guidance for a problem or concern;
- Ask for an Exception Report.

- **Implement**: carry out the necessary corrective actions. Create an Exception Plan on the directive of the Project Board.

At each step update the Issue Register and Issue Report accordingly. Keep the person who raised the issue and who wrote the Issue Report (if different) appraised of its status.

Change Authority. It is the Project Board's responsibility to review and approve requests for change and off-specifications. However this can become quite time consuming. In addition, there is frequently a requirement for specialist knowledge and a significant amount of coordination is required to arrive at the right decisions. Therefore it may be appropriate to delegate some of these considerations to a person or group, called the Change Authority.

For minor changes the Project Manager can be made responsible. In other circumstances a Change Advisory Board (CAB) is installed.

However in all instances when issues are forecast to exceed the agreed tolerances, they should be referred back to the Project Board for decision.

The Change Authority can be allocated a **change budget** to be spent on authorized requests for change. This prevents the costs for implementing changes impacting upon the planned budget for the realization of the project's work. In practice, even without a Change Authority, a change budget can be something that is of interest to the management of the project.

11.6 Responsibilities of the Change theme

For the responsibilities relevant to the Change theme, see table 11.1.

Corporate/programme management	Project Manager (PM)
Provide corporate/programme CMS	• Prepare CMS
	• Manage CM & CC procedures, assisted by Project Support
Executive	• Create and maintain Issue Register, assisted by Project Support
• Approve CMS:	• Ensure TM's implement CM & CC measures
• Set scales for severity & priority	• Implement corrective actions
• Determine change authority/budget	
• Respond to request for advice	**Team Manager (TM)**
• Take decisions on issues	• Implement CM & CC measures
	• Implement corrective actions
Senior User/ Supplier	
• Respond to request for advice	**Project Support**
• Take decisions on Issue Reports	• Maintain Configuration Item Records
	• Assist the PM to maintain Issue Register
Project Assurance	• Assist the PM with CM & CC procedures
• Advice on CMS	• Produce Product Status Accounts
• Advice on examining and solving issues	
• CC = Change Control	
• CM = Configuration Management	
• CMS = Configuration Management Strategy	

Table 11.1 Roles and responsibilities of the Change theme (Based on OGC PRINCE2 material)

Chapter 12
Progress

12.1 Purpose

The purpose of the Progress theme is to establish a mechanism by which to monitor and compare actual achievements against those planned; the purpose is also to provide a forecast for evaluating the project's objectives and its continued viability; and to control any unacceptable deviations.

The Progress theme provides a mechanism for the continued business justification, managing on a stage-by-stage basis and by exception.

12.2 Progress defined

Progress – the measure of the achievements of the objectives of a plan.
Tolerance – the permissible deviation from a plan's objectives without escalating the deviation to the next management level.
Exception – a situation where it is forecast that there will be a deviation beyond the agreed tolerance levels.

Progress controls ensure that for each level of the project management team, the next level of management can:

- Monitor progress;
- Compare achievements against plans;
- Review plans and options against future situations;
- Detect problems and identify risks;
- Initiate corrective actions;
- Authorize further work.

12.3 Management by Exception

- The Project Board meets on decision points only, with intermediate advice and directions when needed;
- The Project Board delegates assurance that the project is being conducted properly to the Project Assurance;
- The Project Board delegates responsibility for the consideration of requests for change to a Change Authority;
- The Project Board delegates the day-to-day management to the Project Manager within set tolerances, with Highlight Reports produced at agreed intervals;
- The Project Manager raises an Exception Report when it is forecast that agreed tolerance levels are likely to be exceeded.

12.4 PRINCE2 approach to Progress

PRINCE2 provides Progress control through:
- Delegating authority;
- Dividing the project in management stages;
- Time- and event-driven progress reporting and reviews;
- Raising exceptions.

12.5 Delegating authority

PRINCE2 recognizes six basic performance areas to be managed. Tolerances have to be defined for each performance area for the respective level of management, see figure 12.1:
- Time, costs and scope tolerances are defined in the Project and Stage Plan and the respective Work Packages;
- Project-level risk tolerances are defined in the Risk Management Strategy. Stage and team-level risk tolerances are defined in the Stage Plans and Work Packages;

- Project-level quality tolerances are defined in the Project Product Description. Product tolerances are defined in the respective Product Descriptions;
- Benefits tolerances are defined in the Business Case.

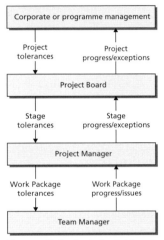

Figure 12.1 The four levels of control (Source: Managing Successful Projects with PRINCE2, produced by OGC)

The main controls for the Project Board are:
- **Authorization** of the initiation, the project and the delivery stages, inclusive of the respective stage tolerances;
- **Progress updates** including Highlight Reports and End Stage Reports;
- **Exceptions and changes** including Issue Reports and Exception Reports.

The main controls for the Project Manager are:
- **Authorization** of the Work Packages and the Work Package tolerances;
- **Progress updates** including Checkpoint Reports and team meetings;
- **Exceptions and changes** including registers and logs.

The project's controls should be documented in the Project Initiation Documentation (PID), the stage controls in the Stage Plan and the controls for the Team Manager in the Work Packages.

12.6 Management stages

Management stages are subdivisions in time, linked to go/no-go decisions with respect to the continuation of the project. Management stages are arranged sequentially.

There are at least two management stages in the project; the initiation stage and the delivery stage. The delivery stage can be split up into more than one management stage. The decision about the number of management stages to be included in the execution stage is taken at the initiation stage.

Technical stages are stages characterized by the application of a set of techniques. Technical stages can overlap. The number of technical stages is normally larger than the number of management stages.

The **number** of management stages depends on:
- How far ahead it is sensible to plan;
- Where the key decisions need to be taken in the project;
- The amount of risk within the project;
- The respective benefits of too many short stages versus too few lengthy ones;
- How confident the Project Board and the Project Manager are in proceeding.

The **length** of the management stages depends on:
- The planning horizon at any point in time;
- The technical stages within the project;

- Alignment with corporate or programme activities;
- The level of risk.

If a management stage ends during a technical stage, it is necessary to split the technical stage up into a part before the go/no-go decision and a part after the go/no-go decision, see figure 12.2.

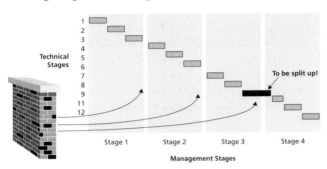

Figure 12.2 Management and technical stages

12.7 Event- and time-driven controls

PRINCE2 recognizes:
- **Event-driven controls** – these take place at the end of a stage (End Stage Report), at the end of the project (End Project Report) or as and when an exception is raised (Exception Report);
- **Time-driven controls** – these take place at predefined periodic intervals, such as Checkpoint Reports and Highlight Reports.

Baselines for progress controls are:
- **Project Plan** – is used by the Project Board to monitor a project's progress on a stage by stage basis;

- **Stage Plan** – is the basis for the day-to-day control by the Project Manager;
- **Exception Plan** – shows actions required to recover from the effect of a tolerance deviation;
- **Work Packages** – authorized by the Project Manager to a Team Manager to undertake project works during a stage.

Reviewing progress:
- **Daily Log** – the personal diary of the Project Manager. This is useful to record actions and also to record problems/ concerns that can be handled informally;
- **Issue Register and Issue Report** – to capture and manage requests for change, off-specifications and other formal issues;
- **Product Status Account** – to provide a status of the products. This is especially of interest if the Project Manager verifies the status and the versions of the products;
- **Quality Register** – to record all planned and implemented quality activities and to act as a pointer to quality records;
- **Risk Register** – to record all identified risks, including the respective risk responses.

Informal records are captured in logs. Formal records are captured in registers.

Capturing and reporting lessons:
- **Lessons Log** – to capture previous lessons from earlier projects and also the lessons learnt during the course of the project itself;
- **Lessons Report** – to forward lessons which will be of interest for other projects. Lessons Reports can be forwarded at stage ends and at project closure.

Reporting on progress:

- **Checkpoint Reports** – produced by the Team Manager at agreed intervals to enable the Project Manager to review Work Package status;
- **Highlight Reports** – produced by the Project Manager at agreed intervals to enable the Project Board to manage by exception between end stage assessments. The Highlight Report can also be sent to other stakeholders as documented in the Communication Management Strategy;
- **End Stage Reports** – produced by the Project Manager at the end of a stage to enable the Project Board to evaluate the previous stage and to authorize the project's continuation;
- **End Project Report** – produced by the Project Manager at the end of the project to enable the Project Board to evaluate the project and authorize project closure.

12.8 Raising exceptions

When it is forecast that agreed tolerances will be exceeded, the appropriate exceptions should be raised to the next management level:

- **Work Package-level exceptions** – the Team Manager has to raise an issue with the Project Manager;
- **Stage-level exceptions** – the Project Manager has to escalate an Exception Report to the Project Board;
- **Project-level exceptions** – the Project Board has to forward the exception report to corporate or programme management for decision.

12.9 Responsibilities of the Progress theme

For the responsibilities that are relevant to the Progress theme, see table 12.1.

Corporate/ programme management	Project Manager (PM)
• Provide project tolerances in mandate • Approve project Exception Plans **Executive** • Provide stage tolerances • Approve stage Exception Plans • Ensure that progress towards the outcome remains consistent from the business perspective • Recommend future actions in project Exception Plans **Senior User** • Ensure that progress towards the outcome remains consistent from the user perspective **Senior Supplier** • Ensure that progress towards the outcome remains consistent from the supplier perspective **Project Assurance** • Monitor changes to the Project Plan in terms of impact on the Business Case • Confirm stage and project progress against agreed tolerances	• Authorize Work Packages • Monitor progress against Stage Plan • Produce Highlight and End Stage Reports • Produce Exception Reports • Maintain project's registers and logs **Team Manager (TM)** • Agree Work Package with PM • Inform Project Support about Quality checks • Produce Checkpoint Reports • Notify PM about forecast deviation from tolerances **Project Support** • Assist with compilation of reports • Contribute with specialist expertise • Maintain Issue, Risk and Quality Register on behalf of the PM

Table 12.1 Roles and responsibilities of the Progress theme (Based on OGC PRINCE2 material)

Chapter 13
Introduction to PRINCE2 processes

PRINCE2 is a process-based approach for project management. There are seven processes in PRINCE2, which provide the set of activities required to direct, manage and deliver a project successfully. A process delivers output(s) for which one or more inputs are needed.

Each process is a structured set of activities that accomplish a specific objective. These activities consist of several recommended actions designed to achieve a typical result. The PRINCE2 processes will be explained in the following chapters. Each process chapter consists of a process diagram with specific elements, as illustrated in table 13.1.

Directing a project	This is a PRINCE2 process, ending with '-ing' (like Starting up or Closing a Project)
Capture previous lessons	This is an activity
Request to initiate a project	This is an event or decision that triggers another process
Project Initiation Documentation	These are management products

Table 13.1 Key to process diagrams in Chapters 14 – 20 (Based on OGC PRINCE2 material)

The seven processes are:
* Starting up a Project;
* Initiating a Project;
* Directing a Project;
* Controlling a Stage;

- Managing Product Delivery;
- Managing a Stage Boundary;
- Closing a Project.

In each of the processes the project is viewed from the Project Manager's perspective, except for Directing a Project (Project Board's perspective) and Managing Product Delivery (Team Manager's perspective), see figure 13.1.

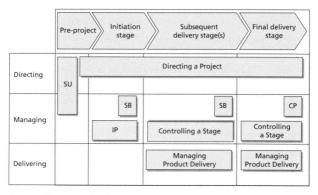

Figure 13.1 Process overview (Source: Managing Successful Projects with PRINCE2, produced by OGC)

(SU = Starting up a Project, IP = Initiating a Project, SB = Managing a Stage Boundary, CP = closing a Project)

13.1 Pre-project

Prior to fully scoping the project, it is essential to verify that the project is worthwhile and viable. The output of Starting up a Project is a Project Brief and a Stage Plan. The Project Board then decides whether to initiate the project.

13.2 Initiation stage

The initiation stage culminates in the production of the Project Initiation Documentation, which is reviewed by the Project Board (in the Directing a Project process) to decide whether to authorize the project. The Managing a Stage Boundary process is used to plan the next stage in detail.

13.3 Subsequent delivery stage(s)

The Project Board delegates day-to-day control to the Project Manager on a stage-by-stage basis. The Project Manager ensures that progress is in line with the stage plan and that the work needed is done by the team (Controlling a Stage process). The team accepts and executes the assigned Work Packages (Managing Product Delivery process). Towards the end of each stage the Project Manager prepares the next stage and requests permission from the Project Board to proceed with the next Stage Plan (Managing a Stage Boundary process).

13.4 Final delivery stage

After execution and approval of all the products, the Project Manager will decommission the project. When the recipients of the project's products are in a position to use and own them on an ongoing basis, the products are transitioned into operational use and the project can be closed. The activities to decommission the project is undertaken by the Closing a Project process.

Chapter 14
Starting up a Project

14.1 Purpose

The purpose of this process is to ensure that the prerequisites for Initiating a Project are in place by answering the question of whether or not the project is considered viable and worthwhile. The Starting up a Project process is a lighter process compared to the more detailed and thorough Initiating a Project process. The aim is to do the minimum necessary in order to decide whether it is worthwhile to even initiate the project.

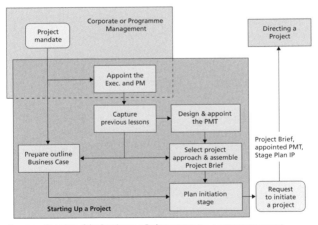

Figure 14.1 Overview of the Starting up a Project process (Based on OGC PRINCE2 material)

14.2 Objectives

The objectives of Starting up a Project are to ensure that:

- There is a business justification, and all the necessary authorities exist for initiating the project;
- There is sufficient information to define and confirm the scope and the approach of the project;
- People are appointed who will execute the initiation stage or have a significant project management role in the project;
- The work for the initiation is planned;
- Time is not wasted initiating a project based on unsound assumptions.

14.3 Context

The trigger for the project is called the project mandate, see Glossary, which is provided by corporate or programme management, as shown in figure 14.1. The mandate is refined to develop the Project Brief, see appendix A.19 and Glossary. The purpose of this is to provide the Project Board with sufficient information to decide whether to initiate the project.

The Project Brief will be refined and extended to the Project Initiation Documentation (created in the Initiating a Project process).

14.4 Activities and recommended actions

The activities within the Starting up a Project process will usually be shared between corporate or programme management, the Executive or the Project Manager.

14.4.1 Appoint the Executive and the Project Manager

To get anything done in the project, a decision maker with the appropriate authority and someone who will manage the project on a day-to-day basis are needed. The following actions are recommended:

- Review the project mandate and check the understanding;
- Appoint the Executive;
- The Executive appoints the Project Manager;
- Create the Daily Log, as a repository for project information.

14.4.2 Capture previous lessons

Previous projects or programmes can provide useful lessons about processes, techniques and estimates for the project. The following actions are recommended:

- Create the Lessons Log;
- Review related Lessons Reports from similar previous projects, programme management, corporate management and external organizations to identify lessons that can be applied to this project;
- Consult people with previous experience of similar projects;
- Record any lessons identified in the Lessons Log.

14.4.3 Design and appoint the project management team

The project requires the right people to make decisions in a timely manner and needs a project management team that reflects the interests of parties involved. The following actions are recommended:

- Review the Lessons Log for lessons related to the project management team structure;
- Design the project management team, including role descriptions and project management team structure, and consider any role combinations;
- Appoint the project management team;
- Estimate the time and effort required for each role and identify potential candidates;
- Confirm the individual candidate's availability and role comprehension and assign the selected people;
- If any risks are identified, add them to the Daily Log.

14.4.4 Prepare the outline Business Case

A crucial element in the project is WHY the project is needed. A high-level view of the Business Case is appropriate at this time. If the project is part of a programme, the Business Case may already have been identified at programme level. The following actions are recommended:

- The Executive drafts the outline Business Case based on what's currently known about the project;
- The Project Manager consults the Executive and Senior User to define what the project is to deliver, and creates the Project Product Description, see appendix A;
- Review the risks captured in the Daily Log and summarize the key risks affecting the project's viability in the outline Business Case.

14.4.5 Select the project approach and assemble the Project Brief

Before any planning activities are undertaken, decisions will be made about how the work is going to be approached. An agreed Project Brief ensures a commonly understood and well-defined start point. The following actions are recommended:

- Evaluate possible delivery solutions and decide upon the approach appropriate to delivering the project product and achieving the outline Business Case;
- Assemble the Project Brief by confirming and incorporating the products from previous activities in this process and by identifying constraints, assumptions, project tolerances, user(s) and any other parties, and the interfaces the project must maintain.

14.4.6 Plan the initiation stage

Initiating a Project needs to be planned and approved, and it takes time and effort to do so. If not, initiation can be aimless and unstructured. The following actions are recommended:

- Based on the approach, decide upon suitable management controls for the project sufficient for it to be initiated;
- Identify the constraints on time and costs for the initiation stage and produce the initiation Stage Plan;
- Review risks in the Daily Log and assess their impact on the Stage Plan for the initiation stage;
- Identify any risks and update the Daily Log;
- Request authorization to initiate the project.

Chapter 15
Directing a Project

15.1 Purpose

The purpose is to enable the Project Board to be accountable for the project's success by making key decisions and exercising overall control, while delegating day-to-day management of the project to the Project Manager.

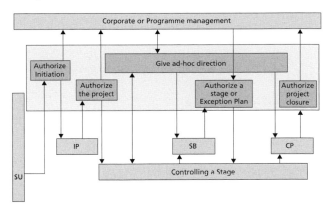

Figure 15.1 Overview of the Directing a Project process (Based on OGC PRINCE2 material)

15.2 Objectives

The objectives of the Directing a Project process are to ensure that:
- There is authority to initiate the project, to deliver the project's products and to close the project;
- Management direction and control are provided throughout the project and that the project remains viable;

- Corporate or programme management has an interface to the project;
- Plans for realizing post-project benefits are managed and reviewed.

15.3 Context

This process views the project from the Project Board's perspective and is triggered by the Project Manager's request to initiate the project, as shown in figure 15.1. The Project Board manages by exception and is informed by the Project Manger via reports and controls on the current situation. The Project Board also communicates with corporate or programme management and assures that there is continued business justification. The Project Board and Project Manager should not only provide formal but also informal communication when needed.

15.4 Activities and recommended actions

15.4.1 Authorize initiation
With this activity the Project Board ensures that the investment that is to be made is worthwhile. The following actions are recommended:

- Review and approve the Project Brief including the Project Product Description and the initiation Stage Plan;
- Verify that the outline Business Case demonstrates a viable project;
- Inform stakeholders and the host site(s) that the project is being initiated and request any required support;
- Authorize the Project Manager to proceed.

15.4.2 Authorize the project
This activity will be triggered by a request from the Project Manager for authorization to deliver the project and should be performed in parallel with the authorization of a Stage or Exception Plan. The following actions are recommended:

- Review and approve the PID and Benefits Review Plan;

- Notify corporate or programme management and other interested parties that the project has been authorized;
- Authorize the Project Manager to deliver the project or to close the project prematurely.

15.4.3 Authorize a Stage or Exception Plan

When a stage nears its end, the Project Board is asked to authorize the next Stage Plan. When an exception has occurred the Project Board may ask the Project Manager to produce an Exception Plan for Project Board approval. The following actions are recommended:

- Review and approve the End Stage Report;
- Review and approve the Stage Plan or Exception Plan;
- Authorize the Project Manager to proceed with the submitted plans;
- Approve the plan and authorize the Project Manager to proceed;
- Communicate the status of the project to corporate or programme management.

15.4.4 Give ad hoc direction

Project Board members may give informal guidance or respond to requests for advice at any time during the project. Triggers for such actions can be:

- Informal requests for advice and guidance;
- An escalated Issue Report;
- An Exception Report;
- The receipt of a Highlight Report;
- Advice and decision from corporate or programme management.

Responses from Project Board (members) can be:

- Assist the Project Manager as required;
- Make a decision within the limits of authority;
- Defer the decision or request more information;
- Instruct the Project Manager to produce an Exception Plan or to close the project prematurely;

- Seek advice from corporate or programme management;
- Keep the project management team and/or corporate or programme management informed.

15.4.5 Authorize project closure

Every project has to end and at that point the Project Board has to assess whether the objectives have been achieved, how the project has deviated from its original plans, or if the project has nothing more to contribute. The following actions are recommended:

- Review the original and current versions of the Project Initiation Documentation and the Project Plan;
- Review and approve the End Project Report;
- Ensure that the post-project benefits review covers the performance of the project, including any possible side-effects;
- Review and gain approval from corporate / programme management for the updated Benefits Review Plan;
- Confirm the updated Business Case;
- Review and issue a project closure notification.

Chapter 16
Initiating a Project

16.1 Purpose

The purpose of this process is to establish solid foundations for the project, enabling the organization to understand the work that needs to be done to deliver the project's products, before committing to a significant spend.

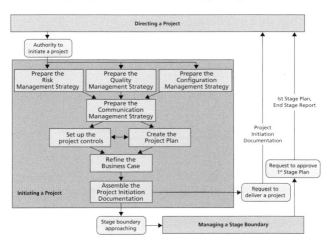

Figure 16.1 Overview of the Initiating a Project process (Source: Managing Successful Projects with PRINCE2, produced by OGC)

16.2 Objectives

The objectives are to ensure there is a common understanding of:
- Why the project is needed, the benefits expected and the associated risks;
- The scope of what is to be done and the products to be delivered;

- How, when and what is to be delivered, and at what cost;
- Who is involved in the project decision making;
- How the required quality will be achieved;
- How baselines will be established and controlled;
- How risks, issues and changes will be identified, assessed and controlled;
- How progress will be monitored and controlled;
- Who needs what information and at what time;
- How the corporate project management method will be tailored to suit the project.

16.3 Context

This process describes how the Project Manager lays down the foundations for a successful project. Therefore all parties must be clear on what, how, when and why.

The process allows the Project Board to authorize the project's continuation. If the process is not undertaken, then the Project Board may be forced to commit significant financial resources without fully understanding how the project's objectives will be achieved.

The Project Manager will create the suite of management products required by the Project Board for control purposes. See figure 16.1.

16.4 Activities and recommended actions

16.4.1 Prepare the Risk, Configuration and Quality Management Strategy

These three strategies describe the goals, the procedures, responsibilities, and tools for the respective aspects of the project, see Product Description

Outlines for the strategies in appendices A.6, A.22 and A.24, or the Glossary in appendix D.

The following actions are recommended:
- Review the Project Brief to understand whether corporate or programme management strategies, standards or practices need to be applied;
- Look for lessons learned;
- Review logs and registers for issues and risks;
- Define the Risk, Configuration and Quality Management Strategies, including procedures, tools and techniques, roles and responsibilities;
- Consult with Project Assurance whether the strategies meet the needs of corporate or programme management;
- Create the Risk Register, initial Configuration Item Records, Issue Register and Quality Register, see appendices A.5, A.12, A,23 and A.25;
- Seek approval from the Project Board.

16.4.2 Prepare the Communication Management Strategy

The Communication Management Strategy is completed last because it may need to include requirements of the other three strategies, see appendix A.4. The following actions are recommended:
- Review the Project Brief to understand whether corporate or programme management strategies, standards or practices need to be applied;
- Look for lessons learnt;
- Review the Risk Register and Daily Log for issues and risks;
- Identify and/or review stakeholders and consult them about their information needs;
- Define the Communication Management Strategy, including communication management procedures, tools and techniques, roles and responsibilities and stakeholder analysis;

- Consult with Project Assurance whether the strategy meets the needs of corporate or programme management;
- Seek approval from the Project Board.

16.4.3 Set up the project controls

The required levels of control between Project Board, Project Manager and Team Manager need to be in place before the project commences its execution. Many controls may have been defined by the strategies but not necessarily put in place, therefore there must be a coherent set. The following actions are recommended:

- With regard to controls, review the Project Brief to understand whether corporate or programme management strategies, standards or practices need to be tailored by PRINCE2;
- Review the four Management Strategies to identify which controls need to be established;
- Look for lessons learned;
- Confirm the project's tolerances and the escalation procedures;
- Summarize the project controls;
- Consult with Project Assurance to assess the project controls;
- Update the Risk Register, Issue Register and/or Daily Log;
- Seek approval from the Project Board.

16.4.4 Create the Project Plan

The timescales and resource requirements are needed for the Project Board's control and the refinement of the Business Case. The Project Manager should undertake this activity with the close involvement of the user(s) and supplier(s). The following actions are recommended:

- Review the Project Brief and look for lessons;
- Review the Risk Register and Issue Register for risks and issues concerning planning;
- Decide on the format and presentation of the Project Plan;
- Identify any planning and control tools to be used;

- Choose the method of estimating;
- Review the four management strategies in order to identify the resources and costs for the project;
- Create a product breakdown structure, product flow diagram and Product Descriptions, see chapter 9 Plans and also appendix C for examples;
- Check if the Project Product Description needs to be updated;
- Create or update the Configuration Item Records for each product to be delivered, see appendix A.5;
- Identify and confirm resources required;
- Identify the effort required for the project controls and include them in the plan;
- Identify risks concerning the plan and document the Project Plan, see appendix A.16 Product Description Plan;
- Get approval from the Project Board.

16.4.5 Refine the Business Case

The outline Business Case needs to be updated with the estimates on time, cost and risks. The detailed Business Case is needed for the Project Board's decision as to whether the project is and remains viable. The following actions are recommended:

- Review the Project Brief and look for lessons;
- Create the detailed Business Case, see appendix A.2;
- Create the Benefits Review Plan, see appendix A.1;
- Get approval from the Project Board.

16.4.6 Assemble the Project Initiation Documentation

All the information on the 'what, why, who, when, where, how, and how much' that is needed for the key stakeholders is collated into the Project Initiation Documentation.

Chapter 17
Controlling a Stage

17.1 Purpose

The purpose of this process is to assign the work to be done, monitor such work, deal with issues, report on progress to the Project Board, and take corrective actions to ensure that the stage remains within tolerance.

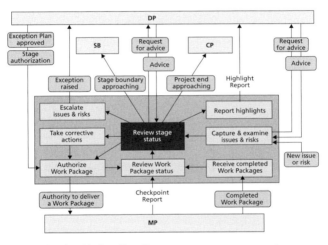

Figure 17.1 Overview of the Controlling a Stage process (based on OGC PRINCE2 material)

17.2 Objectives

The objectives are to ensure that:
*   Attention is focused on the delivery of the stage's products and that uncontrolled change ('scope creep') is avoided;
*   Risks and issues are kept under control;

- The Business Case is kept under review;
- The stage's products are delivered within agreed cost, effort, time and quality, and that they support the achievement of the defined benefits;
- The project management team is focused on delivery within the tolerances laid down.

17.3 Context

This process describes the Project Manager's day-to-day work during each stage.

Where the Project Manager also fulfils the Team Manager's role, the described role of Team Manager may be regarded as the role of an individual team member.

Towards the end of each stage – with the exception of the last one – Managing a Stage Boundary will be invoked. At the end of the final stage, Closing a Project will occur. See figure 17.1.

17.4 Activities and recommended actions

Controlling a stage consists of Work Package-related activities, monitoring and reporting related activities and issue-related activities.

17.4.1 Authorize a Work Package

It would be chaotic if people started activities whenever they thought fit. It is, therefore, important that the work only commences and continues with the consent of the Project Manager. The vehicle for this is the Work Package, see appendix A.26. Triggers for the Project Manager to authorize a Work Package include stage authorization, an approved Exception Plan, a required new Work Package, or a corrective action in response to an issue or risk. The following actions are recommended:

- Examine the current Stage Plan and understand the products, cost, effort and tolerances;
- Examine the PID to understand the required controls, quality standards and how the hand-over of products is to be carried out;
- Define the Work Packages;
- Review the Work Package with the Team Manager and make sure the Team Manager accepts it;
- Review the Team Manager's Team Plan and update the Stage Plan for the timings;
- Update the Quality Register and Configuration Item Records and, if necessary, the Risk Register and Issue Register.

17.4.2 Review Work Package status

A regular assessment of the Work Package is needed. The frequency of this is defined in the agreed Work Package.

The following actions are recommended:

- Collect and review progress information from the Checkpoint Report that relates to the Work Package being executed;
- If necessary, update the Risk Register and Issue Register;
- Update the Stage Plan for the current stage.

17.4.3 Receive completed Work Package

Once the Work Package is completed there should be a confirmation that this is the case. The following actions are recommended:

- Check that the work, as defined in the Work Package, is done and that the Quality Register is complete;
- Ensure that each product in the Work Package is approved and that its Configuration Item Record has been updated;
- Update the status of the Work Package in the Stage Plan.

17.4.4 Review the stage status

To prevent a stage from going out of control, a regular assessment of what has happened and what should have happened is required. The following actions are recommended:

- Review progress for the stage by checking Checkpoint Reports, forecasts and actuals, quality issues, the Risk Register, the status of any corrective actions and resource availability;
- Having analyzed the above, decide if any actions are required, for example authorizing a Work Package, reporting highlights, issues and risks escalation, taking corrective actions, asking the Project Board for advice, or logging any lessons;
- Update the Stage Plan, Risk Register and Issue Register;
- Consider whether to review lessons;
- If the end of stage is approaching, prepare for the next stage (Managing a Stage Boundary);
- If the end of the project is approaching, prepare for Closing a Project.

17.4.5 Report Highlights

The Project Manager has to inform the Project Board and other stakeholders about the progress of the project and stage. The Communication Management Strategy states the required frequency of the Highlight Report, see appendix A.11. The following actions are recommended:

- Assemble the necessary information from Checkpoint Reports, Risk Register, Issue Register, Quality Register, Lessons Log, Product Status Account and any revisions of the Stage Plan for the current reporting period;
- Assemble a list of corrective actions taken during the reporting period;
- Review the Highlight Report for the previous reporting period;
- Produce the current Highlight Report for the current reporting period;
- Distribute the report as stated in the Communication Management Strategy.

17.4.6 Capture and examine issues and risks

Various issues might occur in an ad-hoc manner. There is a need for a consistent way of registering such issues before examining their consequences. The following actions are recommended:

- If the Project Manager can deal with an issue informally, make a note in the Daily Log;
- For issues that need a more formal treatment, check the Configuration Management Strategy for procedures, enter the issue in the Issue Register, categorize it and assess the severity, priority and impact. Create an Issue Report and report the status of the issue and, if needed, inform external parties of it, see chapter 11 Change;
- For risks check the Risk Management Strategy. Enter risks in the Risk Register, identify the risk event, causes and effect. Assess the risk against the plans and Business Case and plan the selected response. Report the status of the risk and, if needed, inform external parties of it, see chapter 10 Risk;
- If necessary take corrective action and ask for advice from the Project Board, or escalate the issue or risk and review the stage status.

17.4.6 Escalate issues and risks

This action applies to all deviations of issues and risks that cannot be resolved within the tolerances set by the Project Board. The following actions are recommended:

- Examine the Stage Plan and Project Plan and extrapolate what would happen if the deviation were allowed to continue;
- Define the options for recovery and assess them against the current Stage Plan and Business Case;
- Describe the situation, options and the recommended action(s) to the Project Board in an Exception Report, see appendix A.10.

17.4.7 Take corrective action

This action applies to all deviations of issues and risks that can be resolved within the tolerances set by the Project Board. The following actions are recommended:

- Collect any relevant information about the deviation;
- Identify and select options to deal with a deviation;
- If needed, authorize a Work Package and update the Configuration Item Records of the products;
- Update the Issue Report, Issue Register and/or Risk Register with the change(s) resulting from the corrective action;
- Update the current Stage Plan.

Chapter 18
Managing Product Delivery

18.1 Purpose

The purpose of this process is to control the link between the Project Manager and the Team Manager(s), by placing formal requirements on accepting, executing and delivering project work.

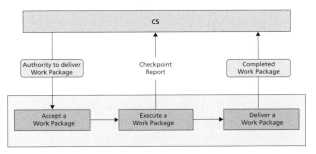

Figure 18.1 Overview of the Managing Product Delivery process (Source: Managing Successful Projects with PRINCE2, produced by OGC)

18.2 Objectives

The objectives of the Managing Product Delivery process are to ensure that:
- Work allocated to the team is authorized and agreed;
- Those involved in a team are clear on the products and the expected effort, cost and timescales;
- The planned products are delivered to expectations and within tolerance;

- Accurate progress information is provided to the Project Manager at an agreed frequency.

18.3 Context

This process views the project from the Team Manager's perspective, as shown in figure 18.1. The Team Manager ensures that the Work Packages are executed and delivered by the team by:

- Accepting and checking authorized Work Packages;
- Ensuring interfaces are maintained;
- Creating a Team Plan, which could vary from a simple appendix to the Work Package to a plan that is constructed in a similar way to the Stage Plan;
- Ensuring that the products are delivered according to agreed development method(s);
- Demonstrating that each product meets its quality criteria;
- Obtaining approval for completed products from the authorities identified in the Product Description;
- Delivering the products to the Project Manager according to any specified procedures in the Work Package.

18.4 Activities and recommended actions

In this process there are three activities, each of which are now described in further detail.

18.4.1 Accept a Work Package

There should be an agreement between the Project Manager and the Team Manager about the aspects of the work to be undertaken. The following actions are recommended:

- Review the Work Package and clarify what is to be delivered, agree upon about constraints, agree the tolerances, understand the reporting

requirements and how approval is obtained and products are to be
handed over, and confirm how the Project Manager will be informed
about completion;
- Produce a Team Plan showing that the product(s) can be delivered
within any given constraints;
- Review any risks against the Team Plan and advise the Project Manager
on any new or modified risks;
- Consult with Project Assurance as to whether any extra reviewers are
needed and – if necessary – update the Quality Register;
- Agree to deliver the Work Package.

18.4.2 Execute a Work Package

While executing the Work Package, the Team Manager should report on
the progress as agreed and should not exceed the permitted tolerances.
Whenever the latter is forecast to happen, the Team Manager needs to raise
an issue. The following actions are recommended:
- Manage the development of the deliverables by addressing effectively
the agreed quality criteria, the required techniques, processes and
procedures, the detailed interfaces and the agreed procedure to update
the Quality Register;
- Log the expended effort;
- Monitor and control any issues, lessons and risks, and advise or notify
the Project Manager of their status and – if needed – raise an issue;
- Obtain approval for the completed deliverables and obtain and issue
approval records and update the Configuration Item Records;
- Review and report on the status of the Work Package to the Project
Manager in Checkpoint Reports.

18.4.3 Deliver the Work Package

Notification of the completion of each Work Package should be passed
through to the Project Manager. The following actions are recommended:
- Review the Quality Register and verify its completion;

- Review the approval records to verify that all the agreed products are approved;
- Update the Team Plan, deliver the products and notify the Project Manager of its completion.

Chapter 19
Managing a Stage Boundary

19.1 Purpose

The purpose of this process is to provide the Project Board with sufficient information so that it can review the success of the current stage, approve the next Stage Plan and review the updated Project Plan. It should also confirm the continued business justification and risk acceptability. In addition, Exception Plans are submitted for approval by the Project Board.

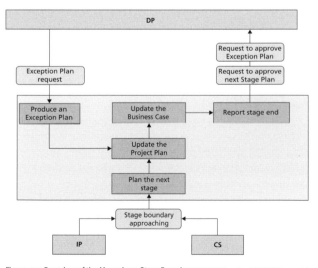

Figure 19.1 Overview of the Managing a Stage Boundary process (based on OGC PRINCE2 material)

19.2 Objectives

The objectives are to:
- Assure the Project Board that the current stage's products are complete and approved;
- Prepare the next Stage Plan;
- Review and – if necessary – update the Project Initiation Documentation;
- Provide the information needed for the Project Board to assess the continuing viability of the project and the aggregated risk exposure;
- Record any lessons that might be applied to future stages or other projects;
- Request authorization to start the next stage.

In case of an exception, the objective is to:
- Prepare an Exception Plan as directed by the Project Board;
- Seek approval to replace the current Project Plan or Stage Plan with the Exception Plan.

19.3 Context

The continuing focus of the project should be confirmed by the Project Board at the end of each (management) stage. Therefore the Project Manager needs to perform various activities to ensure that the Project Board can make the correct decisions, see figure 19.1.

19.4 Activities and recommended actions

19.4.1 Plan the next stage
Near the end of the current stage the Project Manager produces the next Stage Plan, after consultation with Project Board, Project Assurance, Team Managers and other stakeholders. The following actions are recommended:

- Review the elements of the Project Initiation Documentation regarding any required changes;
- Produce the Stage Plan for the next stage, including a review of the Project Plan, the Quality Management Strategy, Risk Register and Issue Register, together with creation or update of the product breakdown structure, Product Descriptions and product flow diagram relating to this next stage;
- Create or update the Configuration Item Records for the products that are to be delivered in this next stage;
- Update the Issue Register and Risk Register for new or modified issues and risks;
- Update the Quality Register for planned quality management activities.

19.4.2 Update the Project Plan

The Project Plan is required to monitor overall progress by the Project Board and is therefore updated to include actuals from the stage about to finish and forecasts from the stage about to commence. The following actions are recommended:

- Check that the current Stage Plan is up-to-date;
- Revise the Project Plan to incorporate current stage actuals, next stage forecasts, any changes to the Project Product Description, any implication of issues and risks, any modified or additional products demanded by the Project Board and any changes within the Project Initiation Documentation;
- If any new risks or issues have been identified, then update the Issue Register and Risk Register.

19.4.3 Update the Business Case

The Project Board is ordinarily only authorized to continue with the project while it remains viable. However projects commonly take place in dynamic environments, therefore there is a need to confirm that they are still viable if/when new insights into costs and end dates have been established. The following actions are recommended:

- Ascertain the aggregated project's risk exposure and identify the key risks that affect the Business Case;
- Update the Benefits Review Plan (if any benefit review has taken place in the current stage);
- Examine and review the Benefits Review Plan, the impact of approved changes that might affect the benefits, the risk profile and key risks, the Issue Register for issues impacting upon the Business Case, the Project Plan to see whether project end dates and/or costs have changed and might, therefore, influence the cost/benefit analysis, and whether any benefit reviews are needed in the next stage;
- If necessary, revise the Business Case and Benefit Review Plan;
- If necessary, update the Issue Register and Risk Register.

19.4.4 Report stage end

This activity should take place as close as possible to the stage end, as is the case with an Exception Plan. The following actions are recommended:

- Review the status of the updated Business Case, the Stage Plan, the team performance, the product performance, the raised issues and risks;
- Prepare an End Stage Report, see appendix A.9, and check the Communication Management Strategy for external interested parties that need a copy of it.

19.4.5 Produce an Exception Plan

Exception Plans are requested by the Project Board in response to an Exception Report. Although an Exception Plan will be produced before the planned stage boundary, the Project Board's approval of it marks a stage boundary for the revised stage. The following actions are recommended:

- Record the issue that has resulted in the Project Board requesting an Exception Plan;

- Review the elements of the Project Initiation Documentation regarding any required changes such as the customer's quality expectations, acceptance criteria, project approach, project management team and role descriptions as well as the usefulness of the strategies and controls. Update the Project Initiation Documentation where needed;
- Produce the Exception Plan:
  - Examine the Stage Plan to define the products to be produced;
  - Examine the Exception Report for details;
  - Examine the Quality Management Strategy if new products need to be produced;
  - Update the product breakdown structure, Product Descriptions and product flow diagram relating to this Exception Plan.
- Create or update the Configuration Item Records for the products to be delivered via the Exception Plan;
- Update the Issue Register and Risk Register for new or modified issues and risks;
- Update the Quality Register for planned quality management activities.

Chapter 20
Closing a Project

20.1 Purpose

The purpose of this process is to provide a point at which acceptance for the project product is confirmed and to verify that approved changes to objectives in the Project Initiation Documentation have been achieved, or that the project has nothing more to contribute.

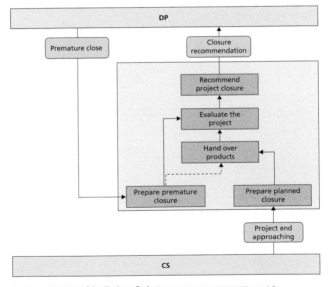

Figure 20.1 Overview of the Closing a Project process (Based on OGC PRINCE2 material)

20.2 Objectives

The objectives of this process are to:
- Verify the user acceptance of the project's products;
- Ensure that the host site is able to support the product;
- Review the project's performance against its baselines;
- Assess any benefits that have been realized, update the forecast of the remaining benefits and plan the review of unrealized benefits;
- Ensure that follow-on action recommendations address all unresolved issues and risks.

20.3 Context

A clear end to a project:
- Is always better than a slow drift into operational use as it is recognized by all parties concerned that the original objectives have been met, the project will soon end, the products can be handed over to operations or a subsequent project or a programme, the project management team will soon disband and the project costs will no longer be incurred;
- Provides an opportunity to identify unachieved goals and objectives so that they can be addressed;
- Transfers ownership from the project management team to the customer.

Triggers can come from a premature closure or a planned closure, as shown in figure 20.1.

20.4 Activities and recommended actions

20.4 1 Prepare planned closure

Before closure will be recommended, the Project Manager must ensure that the expected results have all been achieved and delivered. The following actions are recommended:

- Update the Project Plan with the latest actuals;
- Request a Product Status Account (from Project Support);
- Confirm that the project has delivered all products as agreed and that the acceptance criteria have been met;
- Get approval to notify corporate or programme management that resources will be released.

20.4.2 Prepare premature closure

In situations where the Project Board instructs the Project Manager to close the project prematurely, the Project Manager should ensure that work is not simply abandoned but that the project recovers anything that might be of value, and any gaps that might be due to the project's premature closure are raised with corporate or programme management. The following actions are recommended:

- Update the Issue Register by recording the issue of the premature closure;
- Update the Project Plan with the latest actuals;
- Request a Product Status Account (from Project Support) and determine the status of the products;
- Agree the means for recovering completed products or products in progress;
- Seek approval to give notice to corporate or programme management that resources can be released early.

20.4.3 Hand over products

The project's products will pass on to an operational and maintenance environment before the project is closed. This can either happen at the end of the project in a single release, or in a phased delivery with a number of releases. The following actions are recommended:

- Prepare follow-on action recommendations for products including uncompleted work, issues and risks;
- Check that the Benefits Review Plan includes the post-project confirmation of benefits;
- Examine the Configuration Management Strategy to confirm how products are handed over to the operational and maintenance environment;
- Confirm the acceptance of the products from, and the transfer of the product's responsibility to, the operational and maintenance environment.

20.4.4 Evaluate the project

Successful organizations learn from their project experiences. Therefore there is a need to assess how (un)successful the project has been and what improved estimates might be of help to future projects. The following actions are recommended:

- Review the original intent of the Project Initiation Documentation that was baselined at the time of creation;
- Review the approved changes as defined by the current version of the Project Initiation Documentation;
- Prepare an End Project Report, see appendix A.8;
- Prepare a Lessons Report that can be useful for future projects and get approval from the Project Board to send it to corporate or programme management, see appendix A.15.

20.4.5 Recommend project closure

A closure recommendation should be raised to the Project Board, once the Project Manager has confirmed that the project can be closed. The following actions are recommended:

- Check the Communication Management Strategy for those interested parties that need to know the project is closing;
- Close the project's registers and logs;
- Secure and archive project information to permit a future audit of the performance, actions and decisions of the project management team;
- Prepare and send a project closure notification to the Project Board, stating that the project has closed.

Chapter 21
Tailoring PRINCE2

21.1 What is tailoring?

PRINCE2 is tailored to suit the project's specific project factors as well as environmental factors. Tailoring refers to the appropriate use of PRINCE2 on any given project, so that the correct amount of planning, control, governance and use of the processes and themes are in place.

Embedding, however, refers to the adoption of PRINCE2 across an organization. Table 21.1 sets out the differences between embedding and tailoring.

Embedding	Tailoring
Done by the organization to adopt PRINCE2	Done by the project management team to adapt the method to the context of a specific project
Focus on: • Process responsibilities • Scaling rules / guidance • Standards (templates, definitions) • Training and development • Integration with business processes • Tools • Process assurance	Focus on: • Adapting the themes through the strategies and controls • Incorporating specific terms/language • Revising the Product Descriptions for the management products • Revising the role descriptions for the PRINCE2 project roles • Adjusting the processes to match the above
Guidance in 'PRINCE2 Maturity Model'	Guidance in this pocket guide

Table 21.1 Embedding versus Tailoring (Source: Managing Successful Projects with PRINCE2, produced by OGC)

Tailoring is not just about omitting elements of PRINCE2. Omitting elements will result in the weakening of the project management. Tailoring is more about adapting elements rather than leaving them out.

There is a danger however when PRINCE2 is not tailored. Rigid, 'robotic' or template-driven project management might be the consequence.

21.2 General approach to tailoring

PRINCE2 should be tailored to suit the project's specific project factors as well as environmental factors. As a third aspect the PRINCE2 principles are a Project Manager's guide for how to adapt PRINCE2 without losing its value, see figure 13.1. Because the principles are universal, they will always be applied and are not tailored.

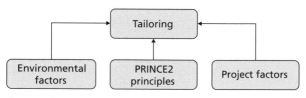

Figure 21.1 Influences on tailoring (Based on OGC PRINCE2 material)

Tailoring consists of the following aspects:
- *Adapting themes* normally consists of incorporating environmental factors, such as relevant corporate or programme policies and standards, and project factors, into the project's strategies and controls;
- *Applying the organization's terms and language* might be of help whenever it improves the understanding of all involved. For example an organization may use the term Progress Report instead of Highlight Report;
- *Adapting the management products* can help when organization-specific parts of their composition offer a better understanding and guidance;
- *Adapting the role descriptions* might be needed because the standard role descriptions are not always suited to an individual's capabilities and authorities;

- *Adapting the processes* can lead to changing the responsibilities for the activities or any reference to standard management products.

To ensure that all the people involved understand the degree of tailoring, it should be clearly stated in the PID how the method is being tailored for that particular project.

21.3 Examples of tailoring

The following sections provide examples and guidance on how to tailor PRINCE2. This must not be seen as an exhaustive list but merely as generic guidance. Each Project Manager should consider the advantages and disadvantages of this guidance in relation to the specific project or environmental factors.

21.4 Projects in a programme environment

Temporary organizations, such as a programme, tend to have a life span that not only covers the completion of projects but also includes the realization of the benefits after the projects have been disbanded. Table 21.2 shows other comparisons between projects and programmes.

Project	Programme
Driven by deliverables	Driven by vision of "end state"
Finite: defined start and finish	No pre-defined path
Bounded and scoped deliverables	Changes to business capabilities
Delivery of product	Coordinated output delivery, including projects not directly delivering benefits
Benefits usually accrue outside the project	Benefits realized as part of the programme and afterwards
Shorter timescale	Longer timescale

Table 21.2 Comparison between projects and programmes (based on OGC PRINCE2 material)

Whenever a project is part of a programme there are some aspects that will require tailoring: themes, processes and management products. In this section the OGC's Managing Successful Programmes (MSP) is the reference for programme management aspects.

When developing the project's Business Case, standards will be defined by the programme. There will be a programme Business Case and therefore the project's Business Case can have a reduced content. In some cases the project's Business Case will be defined by the programme before initiating the project. The project's benefits will be monitored by the programme and the project's Benefit Review Plan might be a part of the programme's benefit realization plan.

Programme and project organizational aspects need to work together in order to enable efficient reporting and reviewing, and ensure that there are clear lines of responsibilities and redundancy is avoided. Some examples of the integration of roles are as follows:
- The programme manager might be the project's Executive;
- The business change manager(s) can fulfil the role of Senior User(s);
- The programme's design authority may also fulfil the role of Project Assurance or Change Authority;
- The programme may fulfil the role of Project Support in their programme support role.

The Programme may provide the Quality Management Strategy. The programme management team may carry out quality control and quality assurance activities as well as provide advice on quality methods.

The project's planning activity should ensure that standards from the programme monitoring and control strategy are adopted. Dependencies with other programme's projects should be taken into account in the project's plan(s).

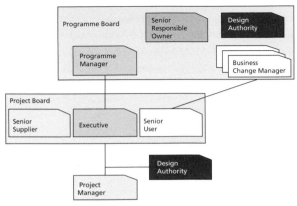

Figure 21.2 Project and Programme roles (Based on OGC PRINCE2 material)

The Risk Management Strategy from the programme should be considered for techniques, scaling or categories in the project.

The programme's issue resolution strategy will be a guide for the project's change control procedures.

In addition, the programme's information strategy will provide guidance for the Configuration Management Strategy.
The programme's monitoring and control strategy will have an influence on the project's reporting and reviewing activities.
Tolerances, stage lengths and the number of stages will also be influenced by the programme.

Starting up a Project is the only project management process that is primarily undertaken by the programme management team. All other project management processes already have a direct interface with (corporate or) programme management.

Consideration should be given to the use of diverse strategy documents for management products: should programme and project documents have the same look and feel or should they differ, and who is responsible for updating the registers and logs and communicating on them?

21.5 Project scale

The scale of a project is not only related to the size of it but also to the context of the project's complexity, risk and importance, see table 21.3. Nevertheless all the PRINCE2 principles should be considered, rather than looking at what principles not to use. Using PRINCE2 can be regarded as a way of reducing project failure. Therefore, whenever an element of PRINCE2 is relaxed, this should be regarded as taking a risk.

Project scale	Characteristics	Applying PRINCE2
High ↑	• Programme • Business transformation	• MSP in programme, PRINCE2 in projects
	• Daunting project • High risk, cost, importance visibility • Multiple organizations • International	• Multiple delivery stages • Extended Project Board • Separate TMs and Project Support • Individual management products
	• Normal projects • Medium risk, cost, importance, visibility • Multiple site	• One or more delivery stages • Standard Project Board • Separate role TM & Project Support optional • Some management products combined
	• Simple project • Low risk, cost, importance, visibility • Single organization • Single site	• Single delivery stage • Simple Project Board • PM fulfils TM & Project Support role • Combined management products
↓ **Low**	• Task • Simple person Project Board • PM is also carrying out the work • Costs within "business as usual" budget • Straightforward business justification/instruction	• Work Package delivery

Table 21.3 Examples of projects of different scales (Based on OGC PRINCE2 material)

Looking at the themes, the following considerations should be taken into account for *simple projects*:

- Roles should be combined, not eliminated, e.g. Project Manager could combine Project Support and Team Manager. Another example is the combination of the Executive and Senior User role(s);
- A Business Case for simple projects can be any documentation of the business justification;
- Product Descriptions and a simple plan can be sufficient;
- A simple understanding of quality levels is required;
- Risk analysis, risk actions and risk reporting can be achieved via a simple form;
- A simple method of change control can be adopted;
- A short written or oral report can be utilised.

All of the processes are relevant in simple projects. In some cases it might be appropriate to handle Starting up a Project in a less formal way, or to combine Starting up a Project and Initiating a Project.

Guidance on management products in small or simple projects include:

- The Project Board can receive oral reports or have a verbal exchange of information;
- Reports could even be produced in the form of an email;
- The Project Initiation Documentation could be a set of presentation slides;
- Small projects can be managed by four sets of documents: Project Initiation Documentation (including the Project Brief), Highlight Report, Daily Log (including risks, issues etc.) and the End Project Report (including lessons);
- When there is only one delivery stage, a Stage Plan and an End Stage Report are redundant;
- If there are no Team Manager(s) then a Work Package and Checkpoint Reports might not be of use;

- An Issue Register or Daily Log with all issues in it can be more useful than an Issue Report for every issue.

21.6 Commercial customer/supplier environment

If there is a commercial relationship between the customer and the supplier, the main consideration is that there are at least two (one for the customer and one for the supplier) sets of reasons to undertake the project, management systems, governance structures and corporate cultures.

The customer and the supplier will each have their own Business Case as well. If one of these Business Cases is no longer valid, the project will struggle and will most likely fail, even if the other party's Business Case is still relevant. Each party's Business Case, however, is often (partly) kept private from the other.

The appointment of the Senior Supplier role is a key decision in a commercial relationship. Should the supplier fulfil that role himself or should a contract manager be employed? And what if there is more than one supplier? It is advisable to appoint a prime contractor as Senior Supplier when there are more than four suppliers. When there is a procurement stage within the project, a senior person from procurement may fulfil this role until the supplier is selected.

The Project Manager will – in most cases – come from the customer, whereas the supplier fulfils the role of Team Manager. When the project is managed from within the supplier organization, the Project Manager can be from the supplier side. However who is going to be the Senior User? It could be an option to appoint the account manager as Senior User, since he or she fulfils the role of making decisions on behalf of the customer.

These approaches have to be defined in terms of whether they will conform to the customer's strategy, the supplier's strategy, or a combination of the two.

If the project is managed stage-by-stage, then a contractual solution for the project as a whole can be found in the adoption of stage-by-stage payments. In this situation the supplier's Team Plan can remain private from the customer. A good Checkpoint Report forms the basis upon which the Project Manager then can perform the monitoring and control aspects.

Risk Registers might also remain private, since some risks are unique to only one of the parties. Whenever there is a joint Risk Register, care should be taken as to who is the risk owner.

The change control procedure should align with the customer's purchasing procedures and supplier's approval procedures. The means of reporting on the progress of the project or stage should align with the organization's governance requirements, if they are in place.

On the supplier's side the processes should be tailored: Starting up a Project will take place at a pre-contract level as a response to the customer's request for proposal. Initiating a Project, however, will end with an approval of the contract and an authorization of the project by the Project Board.

The Project Initiation Documentation should focus on the liabilities and contractual obligations. For the external supplier a Work Package may be viewed as a legal contract.

21.7 Multi-organization projects

When there are more than two organizations involved, such as is the case with joint ventures and inter-departmental or inter-governmental projects, there is a situation of multi-ownership. The guidance in such cases is similar to the commercial customer/supplier environment. The term 'contract' could be substituted by 'agreement'. However one should take care that Project Boards do not become too large and unwieldy for effective decision making.

21.8 Project type

Not only is size of the project or the issue of relationships important as far as tailoring is concerned. The type of project also influences the application of PRINCE2.

21.8.1 Lifecycle models

There are other types of methods that focus on the delivery and verification of specialist products such as waterfall or agile methods (e.g. DSDM Atern). PRINCE2 deliberately does not address these aspects and, therefore, needs to be tailored in the following ways in order to work alongside these specialist lifecycle models:

- Aligning the management stages to the development lifecycle (e.g. design, build, test, hand-over);
- Using the tolerances, like narrow tolerances for time and quality, and a wider tolerance for scope, when utilising an agile or iterative model;
- Integrating specialist roles in the project management team. Very often the struggle is to decide what these roles are called. More importantly, however, the responsibilities should be clear so that they are understood by all involved;

- Lifecycle models can prescribe project management products. It is important in such cases to avoid duplication or gaps. The sensible approach is to decide whether to use the PRINCE2 equivalent or not.

21.8.2 The evolving project

Projects involving research and development, development of a new policy or a feasibility study are typical of evolving projects: projects without a predefined specification but more evolving specifications as the project progresses. Very often these specifications are contestable and negotiable during the project lifecycle. The PRINCE2 Business Case in such cases is handled as a 'best and agreed forecast' which will evolve during the project's lifecycle.

21.8.3 The feasibility project

A feasibility study, see figure 21.3, may be needed to investigate the situation and develop the options to proceed. Such a study is a project in itself, since the preferred option to proceed will have a different Business Case, Project Plan and/or risks.

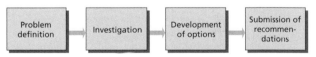

Figure 21.3 Feasibility activities (Source: Managing Successful Projects with PRINCE2, produced by OGC)

At the end of the feasibility study there should be one product: the recommendation. The decision to proceed or not should follow after the recommendation. Policy projects are similar to feasibility projects, the output has no direct value other than to make a reliable decision. Implementing the agreed recommendation is another project.

21.9 Sector differences

There are, of course, differences between the public and the private sectors. The need for a Business Case is not disputed. However, within the UK public sector there are two aspects that require the tailoring of PRINCE2:

1. *There is a Senior Responsible Owner (SRO):* in such cases, as in the UK government sector where the SRO is used increasingly, there are two considerations. Firstly in a programme context the project's Executive reports to the SRO, who is appointed as part of the programme. Secondly whenever an SRO is appointed in a single project, this person can fulfil the role of Executive or appoint someone who fulfils this role.

2. *The project is subject to OGC Gateway review:* the OGC Gateway review is best practice in the UK public sector. It delivers a 'peer review' in which independent practitioners from outside the project use their experience and expertise to examine the progress and the likelihood of successful delivery. PRINCE2 aligns with these gateway reviews as follows:

   • The Directing a Project activity that authorizes initiation aligns with Review 1: business justification;

   • The Directing a Project activity that authorizes a Stage or Exception Plan aligns with Reviews 2, 3 and 4: delivery strategy, investment decision and readiness for service.

21.10   Bodies of Knowledge

There is a difference between a Body of Knowledge (BoK) and PRINCE2, see table 21.4. Examples include the IPMA Competency Baseline(s), PMI's PMBOK or the APM's Body of Knowledge (APMBOK). Actually these are complementary.

PRINCE2	Body of Knowledge
• A project management method • Prescriptive • Integrated set of processes and themes • Covers all PMT roles • Does not cover personal skills • References techniques	• A broad collection of 'good practice' for project management • Non-prescriptive • Each topic can be referred in isolation • Targeted at Project Managers • Covers interpersonal skills • Describes techniques

Table 21.4 Comparison between PRINCE2 and Bodies of Knowledge

PRINCE2 provides *what* needs to be done, *when* and by *whom*. Bodies of Knowledge are merely there to point out techniques that assist in *how* those things can be done.

If an organization is aligned to any of these BoKs, tailoring PRINCE2 should consist of agreeing one set of terms to apply and aligning the management products with those recommended by the BoK.

Appendix A
Outline Product Descriptions for the management products

A.1 Benefits Review Plan

A Benefits Review Plan defines how and when measurement of the achievements of the project's benefits can be made.

Composition

- What benefits are to be measured;
- Who is accountable for the expected benefits;
- How and when can the benefits be measured;
- What resources are needed for the review;
- Baselines measures;
- How the performance of the product will be reviewed.

A.2 Business Case

A Business Case documents the justification for undertaking the project based on the estimated costs and the expected benefits.

Composition

- Executive summary;
- Reasons;
- Business options;
- Expected benefits and the benefit tolerances;
- Expected dis-benefits;
- Timescale;
- Costs;

- Investment appraisal;
- Major risks.

A.3   Checkpoint Report

The Checkpoint Report is used by the Team Manager to report on the status of the Work Package to the Project Manager at a frequency that is defined in the Work Package.

Composition
- Date;
- Period;
- Follow-ups;
- This reporting period, covering products completed and being developed, quality management activities and lessons identified;
- The next reporting period, covering products to be completed and to be developed, and quality management activities;
- Status of the Work Package tolerance;
- Issues and risks.

A.4   Communication Management Strategy

The Communication Management Strategy describes the frequency and means of communication to all parties involved. It facilitates stakeholder engagement.

Composition
- Introduction;
- Communication procedure;
- Tools and techniques;
- Records;
- Reporting;
- Timing of communication activities;
- Roles and responsibilities;
- Stakeholder analysis:

- – Identification of each interested party;
- – Current relationship;
- – Desired relationship;
- – Interfaces;
- – Key messages.
- Information needs of each interested party:
  - – Information required to be provided from the project;
  - – Information required to be provided to the project;
  - – Information provider;
  - – Frequency, means and format of communication.

A.5   Configuration Item Record

The Configuration Item Record makes it possible to record information such as history, status, version, variant and any relationship between them.

The actual composition is defined in the Configuration Management Strategy, see appendix A.6. The set of Configuration Item Records is called a configuration library.

Composition

The suggested content of a Configuration Item Record is as follows:

- Project identifier;
- Item identifier;
- Current version;
- Item title;
- Date of last change;
- Owner;
- Location;
- Copy holders;
- Item type;
- Item attributes;
- Stage;

- Users;
- Status;
- Product state;
- Variant;
- Producer;
- Date allocated;
- Source;
- Relationship with other items;
- Cross-references with issues, risks and documents.

A.6   Configuration Management Strategy

A Configuration Management Strategy identifies how, when and by whom the products will be controlled and secured.

Composition
- Introduction;
- Configuration management procedure (including the planning, identification, control, status accounting and verification and audit activities);
- Issue and change control procedure (including capturing, examining, proposing, deciding and implementing activities);
- Tools and techniques;
- Definition of the content of the Issue Register, see appendix A.12, and the Configuration Item Records, see appendix A.5;
- Composition of the Issue Report, see appendix A.13, and Product Status Account;
- Timing of configuration management and issue and change control activities;
- Roles and responsibilities;
- Scales for prioritizing requests for change and off-specification and severity, in terms of the level of management that can decide on these issues.

A.7   Daily Log

The Daily Log records informal issues, actions or events not covered by any other PRINCE2 registers or logs. It is the Project Manager's diary. It is also used as a repository for issues and risks during Starting up a Project.

Composition
- Date of entry;
- Problem, action, event or comment;
- Person responsible;
- Target date;
- Results.

A.8   End Project Report

The End Project Report indicates how the project performed against the Project Initiation Documentation. It passes the following details on to the group charged with the future support: any useful lessons, details of unfinished work, ongoing risks, or potential product modifications.

Composition
- Project Manager's report on the project's performance;
- Review of the Business Case;
- Review of the project's objectives;
- Review of team performance;
- Review of:
  - Quality records;
  - Approval records;
  - Off-specifications;
  - Project product handover;
  - Summary of follow-on action recommendations.
- Lessons Report, see appendix A.15.

A.9   End Stage Report

An End Stage Report contains sufficient information for the Project Board to decide what action to take on the project during a stage boundary.

Composition

- Project Manager's report on the stage's performance;
- Review of the Business Case;
- Review of project and stage objectives;
- Review of the stage's objectives;
- Review of team's performance;
- Review of:
  - Quality records;
  - Approval records;
  - Off-specifications;
  - Project product handover (if applicable);
  - Summary of follow-on action recommendations (if applicable).
- Lessons Report, see appendix A.15;
- Summary of the current risks and issues;
- Forecast for project and next stage.

When an End Stage Report is produced at the end of the initiation stage, not all of the above elements are required.

A.10   Exception Report

An Exception Report is produced by the Project Manager when a Stage Plan or Project Plan is forecast to exceed its tolerance levels.

Composition

- Exception title;
- Cause of the exception;
- Consequences of the deviation for the project and/or programme;

- Options and the effect of each option on the Business Case, risks and tolerances;
- Recommendations;
- Lessons.

For urgent exceptions it is recommended that in the first instance the Exception Report is oral, and this is then followed by completion of the agreed form.

A.11   Highlight Report

The Project Manager uses the Highlight Report to provide the Project Board and other stakeholders with a summary of the status of a stage at a defined frequency.

Composition

- Date;
- Period;
- Stage status summary;
- This reporting period, covering the status of Work Packages, products completed, products planned but not started or completed in the period and any corrective actions;
- The next reporting period, covering the status of Work Packages, products to be completed and any corrective actions to be carried out;
- Project and stage tolerance status;
- Requests for change;
- Key issues and risks;
- Lessons Report, if appropriate, see appendix A.15.

A.12   Issue Register

The Issue Register contains information on all formally managed issues and the Project Manager should monitor it on a regular basis.

Composition

Each record in the Issue Register should contain the following:

- Issue identifier;
- Issue type (being a request for change, off-specification or problem/concern);
- Date raised;
- Raised by;
- Issue Report author, see appendix A.13;
- Issue description (with cause and effect);
- Priority (to be re-evaluated after impact-analysis);
- Severity (to indicate the required management level to make a decision);
- Status;
- Closure date.

A.13　Issue Report

An Issue Report contains the description, impact assessment and recommendations for each formally handled issue (request for change, off-specification or problem/concern).

Composition

- Issue identifier (unique reference to Issue Register, see appendix A.12);
- Issue type (request for change, off-specification or problem/concern);
- Date raised;
- Raised by;
- Issue Report author;
- Issue description (with cause and effect);
- Impact analysis;
- Recommendation;
- Priority (to be re-evaluated after impact-analysis);
- Severity (to indicate the required management level to make a decision);

- Decision;
- Approved by;
- Decision date;
- Closure date.

A.14 Lessons Log

The Lessons Log is a repository for lessons (both good and bad experiences) that can be applied to this or future projects. Some lessons originate from previous projects, whilst other lessons originate from within the current project.

Composition
- Lesson type (for this project, corporate or programme, or both);
- Lesson detail (event, effect, cause or trigger, warning indicators, recommendations, or whether the event was previously identified as a risk);
- Date logged;
- Logged by;
- Priority.

A.15 Lessons Report

The Lessons Report is used to pass on any lessons to other projects. Typically a Lessons Report is included in the End Stage Report, see appendix A.9, or End Project Report, see appendix A.8. Information can be used to improve standards or future estimating.

Composition
- Executive summary;
- Scope of the report (stage or project);
- Review of what went well, what went badly and any resultant recommendations about the following:

- Project management method;
- Specialist methods;
- Project strategies;
- Project controls;
- Abnormal events causing deviations.
- Review of useful measurements of:
  - Effort to create products;
  - Effectiveness of the Quality Management Strategy;
  - Issue and risk statistics.
- For significant lessons it may be useful to have detailed information on event, effect, cause or trigger, recommendations, if there were warning indicators, or whether the event was previously identified as a risk.

A.16   Plan

A plan is a statement of how and when objectives are to be achieved. It shows therefore the major products, activities and resources (for a description of all the plans, see section 9.2.).

Composition
- Plan description (plan level and approach);
- Plan prerequisites (aspects that must be in place and remain in place for the project to be successful);
- External dependencies;
- Planning assumptions;
- Lessons incorporated;
- Monitoring and control;
- Budgets (including provisions for risks and changes);
- Tolerances (time, cost and scope);
- Product Descriptions, see appendix A.17, with quality tolerances;
- Schedule with graphical representation of:
  - Gantt or bar chart;

- Product breakdown structure and product flow diagram, see appendix C for examples;
- Activity network;
- Table of resource requirements;
- Table of requested/assigned resources by name.

A.17   Product Description

Product Descriptions can be used to assist in understanding all relevant aspects of the product and defining the user of the product, see appendix C for an example of a product based planning.

Composition
- Identifier;
- Title;
- Purpose (the purpose that the product will fulfil);
- Composition (list of parts);
- Derivation (sources);
- Format and presentation (characteristics);
- Development skills required;
- Quality criteria (reference to standards and/or unique specifications);
- Quality tolerance (range to be acceptable);
- Quality method;
- Quality skills required;
- Quality responsibilities.

A.18   Product Status Account

The Product Status Account provides information about the status of products in the project, stage or any particular area.

Composition

- Report scope (project, stage or a particular area);
- Date produced;
- Product status – for each product it may include:
  - Product identifier and title;
  - Version;
  - Status and date of status change;
  - Product state;
  - Owner;
  - Copy-holders;
  - Location;
  - User(s);
  - Producer and date allocated to producer;
  - Planned and actual dates that Product Description and product were baselined;
  - Planned date for the next baseline;
  - List of related items;
  - List of related issues and risks.

A.19   Project Brief

The Project Brief is used to provide a full and firm foundation for the initiation of the project.

Composition

- Project definition, which includes:
  - Background;
  - Project objectives (containing time, cost, quality, scope, risk and benefit performance goals);
  - Desired outcomes;
  - Project scope and exclusions;
  - Constraints and assumptions;

- – Project tolerances;
- – The user(s) and any other known interested parties;
- – Interfaces.
- Outline Business Case (reasons why and the business option selected);
- Project Product Description, see appendix A.21;
- Project approach (choice of solution to be used);
- Project management team structure (chart);
- Role descriptions;
- References.

A.20   Project Initiation Documentation

The purpose of the Project Initiation Documentation is to define the project, so that the project's overall success can be managed and assessed. It forms a contract between the Project Board and the Project Manager. There are three primary uses for this documentation: (1) to ensure there is a sound basis before asking the Project Board to make any significant commitment to the project; (2) to act as a base document against which progress, issues and viability can be assessed; (3) to provide a single source of reference for staff joining the project organization.

Its elements should be updated and re-baselined as and when necessary. The version of the Project Initiation Documentation that provided authorization for the project is preserved to act as reference for assessing the performance when closing the project.

Composition

- Project Definition, which includes:
  - – Background;
  - – Project objectives and desired outcomes;
  - – Project scope and exclusions;

- – Constraints and assumptions;
- – The user(s) and any other known interested parties;
- – Interfaces.
- Project approach;
- Business Case, see appendix A.2, the project's justification based on estimated cost, time, risks and benefits;
- Project management team structure;
- Role descriptions;
- Quality Management Strategy, see appendix A.22;
- Configuration Management Strategy, see appendix A.6;
- Risk Management Strategy, see appendix A.24;
- Communication Management Strategy, see appendix A.4;
- Project Plan, see appendix A.16;
- Project controls (for a summary see chapter 12);
- Tailoring PRINCE2, see chapter 21.

A.21   Project Product Description

A Project Product Description is a special form of Product Description for the project product. It defines what is to be delivered in order to gain acceptance. The Project Product Description is created during the Starting up a Project process, refined during the Initiating a Project process, and is subject to formal change control. At the end of the project it is used to check whether the project has delivered what was expected.

Composition
- Title;
- Purpose (of the project product and who will use the project product);
- Composition (major products);
- Derivation (source products such as existing products to be modified, design specifications, feasibility report, or the project mandate);
- Development skills required;

- Customer's quality expectations (the expected quality of the project product and the required standards and processes to achieve that quality);
- Acceptance criteria (prioritized list of criteria that must be met by the project product before customer's acceptance);
- Project-level quality tolerances;
- Acceptance method (the means by which acceptance is confirmed);
- Acceptance responsibilities.

A.22   Quality Management Strategy

The Quality Management Strategy is used to define the quality techniques, standards and quality responsibilities required to achieve the specified levels of quality.

Composition
- Introduction;
- Quality management procedure:
  - Quality planning;
  - Quality control (standards to use, templates and forms, quality methods, metrics to apply);
  - Quality assurance (Project Board's responsibilities, compliance audits or corporate / programme reviews).
- Tools and techniques;
- Records (for example format of the Quality Register, see appendix A.23);
- Reporting (what reports, their purpose, timing and recipients);
- Timing of quality management activities;
- Roles and responsibilities.

A.23   Quality Register

The Quality Register is used to summarize all past and future quality management activities. Information from the Quality Register is used in the End Stage Report(s) and End Project Report(s).

Composition
Each record in the Quality Register should include the following:
- Quality identifier;
- Product identifier(s);
- Product title(s);
- Method;
- Roles and responsibilities;
- Planned, forecast and actual dates for quality activities and sign-off;
- Result (of the quality activities);
- Reference to quality records.

A.24   Risk Management Strategy

The Risk Management Strategy describes how risk management will be embedded within the project management activities.

Composition
- Introduction;
- Risk management procedure (if the procedure varies from the corporate or programme standards, the variance should be justified). It covers activities such as identify, assess, plan, implement and communicate;
- Tools and techniques;
- Records (format and composition);
- Reporting (what reports, their purpose, timing and recipients);
- Timing of risk management activities;

- Roles and responsibilities;
- Scales (for estimating probability and impact);
- Proximity (e.g. imminent, in the current stage, in this project, after the project);
- Risk categories;
- Risk response categories, see section 10.5;
- Early-warning indicators;
- Risk tolerance (the levels of risk exposure which, when exceeded, require the risk to be escalated to the next level of management);
- Risk budget (how to use it).

A.25   Risk Register

The purpose of the Risk Register is to capture and maintain the information on all the identified risks related to the project.

Composition

Each record in the Risk Register should contain the following:
- Risk identifier;
- Risk author;
- Date registered;
- Risk category;
- Risk description;
- Probability, impact and expected value;
- Proximity;
- Risk response categories;
- Risk response;
- Risk status;
- Risk owner;
- Risk actionee.

A.26   Work Package

A Work Package is a set of information on one or more products. By authorizing and accepting a Work Package the responsibility for the Work Package passes on from the Project Manager to the Team Manager or team members.

Composition

The content may vary depending on the project:

- Date;
- Team Manager or person authorized;
- Work Package description;
- Techniques, processes and procedures to use;
- Development interfaces;
- Operations and maintenance interfaces;
- Configuration management requirements;
- Joint agreements (on effort, cost, time and milestones);
- Tolerances (cost, time, scope and/or risk);
- Constraints;
- Reporting arrangements;
- Problem handling and escalation;
- Extracts from Stage Plan;
- Reference to Product Description(s);
- Approval method.

Appendix B
Roles and responsibilities

B.1 Executive

The Executive is ultimately responsible for the success of the project, supported by the Senior User(s) and the Senior Supplier(s). The Executive has to ensure that the project is achieving its objectives and is delivering the project product, so enabling the forecasted benefits to be attained. The Executive is responsible for the Business Case.

Derived from this, the Executive is responsible for:
- Designing and appointing the project management team;
- Overseeing the development of the Project Brief;
- Ensuring alignment with corporate or programme strategies;
- Overseeing the development of the Business Case;
- Securing the funding for the project;
- Approving any supplier contract if the relationship between customer and supplier is a commercial one;
- Organizing and chairing Project Board reviews;
- Holding the Senior User to account for realizing the benefits, and ensuring that benefits reviews take place to monitor the extent to which benefits are achieved;
- Holding the Senior Supplier to account for the quality and integrity of the specialist approach and specialist products;
- Monitoring and controlling the progress of the project at strategic level, in particular reviewing the Business Case on a regular basis;
- Ensuring that issues and risks associated with the Business Case are identified, assessed and controlled;
- Taking decisions on escalated issues and risks, with continued focus on business justification;

- Escalating issues and risks to corporate or programme management if project tolerances are forecast to be exceeded;
- Transferring responsibility for post-project benefits reviews to corporate or programme management.

B.2　Senior User

The Senior User represents the interests of all those who will use the project's product. The Senior User specifies the benefits and is held to account by demonstrating to corporate or programme management that the forecast benefits have in fact been realized.

Derived from this, the Senior User is responsible for:
- Developing the customer quality expectations and acceptance criteria for the project;
- Ensuring that the project's products will deliver the desired outcome and meet user requirements;
- Ensuring that the project's products will be monitored against user requirements;
- Ensuring that the user resources which are required are made available;
- Resolving user requirements and conflicts of priority;
- Making decisions on issues with a focus on safeguarding the expected benefits;
- Briefing and advising user management on all matters relating to the project;
- Undertaking Project Assurance from the user point of view;
- Ensuring that the expected benefits are realized;
- Providing a statement of 'actual' versus 'forecast' benefits at benefits reviews;
- Maintaining business performance stability during the transition of the project's product into business operations.

B.3   Senior Supplier

The Senior Supplier represents the interests of all those who design, develop, facilitate, produce and implement the project's products. This role is accountable for the quality of the products delivered by the supplier(s) and is responsible for the technical integrity of the project.

Derived from this, the Senior Supplier is responsible for:
- Assessing and confirming the viability of the project's approach;
- Ensuring that the proposals for designing, developing, facilitating, producing and implementing are realistic;
- Advising on the selection of the acceptance methods;
- Ensuring quality procedures are used correctly;
- Ensuring that the supplier resources which are required are made available;
- Resolving supplier requirements and conflicts of priority;
- Briefing non-technical management on supplier aspects;
- Deciding on issues with a focus on safeguarding supplier interests;
- Briefing and advising supplier management on all matters relating to the project;
- Undertaking Project Assurance from a supplier perspective.

B.4   Project Manager

The Project Manager has the authority to run the project on a day-to-day basis on behalf of the Project Board. The Project Manager's prime responsibility is to ensure that the project delivers the required products within the specified tolerances and is capable of achieving the benefits defined in the Business Case.

Derived from this, the Project Manager is responsible for:

- Preparing the Project Brief;
- Preparing the PID and its components;
- Preparing the Benefits Review Plan;
- Preparing the Project, Stage and Exception Plans;
- Preparing and authorizing Work Packages;
- Creating and maintaining the Issue and Risk Registers;
- Creating and maintaining the Daily and Lessons Logs;
- Liaising with Project Assurance;
- Liaising with external suppliers and account managers;
- Leading and motivating the project team;
- Supervising the Project Support;
- Managing the information flow between the directing and delivering processes;
- Producing the project and stage-level reports;
- Managing the production and integration of the project's products, the overall progress, the use of resources and the initiating of corrective actions when necessary;
- Establishing, implementing and verifying the identified strategies;
- Implementing and maintaining the Issue and Configuration Management procedures;
- Establishing and managing the project controls;
- Advising the Project Board of any deviation from the plan.

B.5   Team Manager

The Team Manager's prime responsibility is to ensure production of the assigned products to an appropriate quality and within the tolerances agreed. The Team Manager reports within the project to the Project Manager.

Derived from this, the Team Manager is responsible for:

- Preparing the Team Plan and agreeing the Work Package;
- Planning, monitoring and managing the team's work;
- Taking responsibility for the progress of the work and the use of resources, and taking corrective actions when necessary;
- Liaising with Project Assurance and Project Support;
- Ensuring appropriate entries are made in the Quality Register;
- Producing the Checkpoint Reports;
- Identifying and advising the Project Manager of any issues and risks associated with the Work Package;
- Advising the Project Manager of any deviations from the plan, recommending corrective actions and helping to prepare appropriate Exception Plans;
- Assisting the Project Manager in examining issues and risks;
- Managing issues and risks assigned by the Project Manager;
- Passing back the completed Work Package to the Project Manager.

B.6   Project Assurance

The prime responsibility of Project Assurance is to undertake assurance in relation to the execution and performance of the project on behalf of the individual members of the Project Board.

Derived from this, the responsibilities of Business Assurance are:

- Assisting in the development of the Business Case and Benefits Review Plan;
- Advising on the selection of project management team members;
- Ensuring liaison between business, user and supplier;
- Advising on the Risk Management Strategy;
- Periodically checking that the project remains viable and remains aligned with corporate or programme strategies;
- Reviewing the project's finance;

- Checking that contractor payments are authorized;
- Verifying that solutions are providing value for money;
- Ensuring issues and risk are identified and managed correctly;
- Assessing that aggregate risk remains within tolerance;
- Monitoring progress against plan and tolerances.

The responsibilities of User Assurance are:
- Advising on stakeholder engagement;
- Ensuring that the appropriate people are involved in documenting the Product Descriptions, and that the specifications of users' needs are accurate, complete and unambiguous;
- Assessing whether the solution will meet users' needs and is progressing towards that target;
- Ensuring quality activities have proper users' representation;
- Ensuring that user liaison is functioning effectively;
- Advising on the impact of issues from a user perspective;
- Monitoring risks to the users.

The responsibilities of Supplier Assurance are:
- Reviewing the Product Descriptions;
- Advising on Quality and Configuration Management Strategy;
- Advising on the project approach and methods;
- Ensuring that the supplier and operating standards are defined, met and used to good effect;
- Ensuring the scope of the project is not changed unnoticed;
- Ensuring that quality control procedures are adhered to correctly;
- Advising on the impact of issues from a production perspective;
- Monitoring risks associated with the production aspects of the project.

B.7   Change Authority

The major responsibility of the Change Authority is to undertake reviews of requests for change and off-specifications on behalf of the Project Board. The Project Manager could be assigned as the Change Authority for some aspects of the project.

Derived from this, the responsibilities of the Change Authority are:
*   Reviewing and approving or rejecting all requests for change and off-specifications within the delegated limits of authority and change budget set by the Project Board;
*   Referring to the Project Board if any delegated limits of authority or allocated change budget are forecast to be exceeded.

B.8   Project Support

The responsibilities of the Project Support can vary depending upon the project, the Project Manager and the project environment. The Project Support supports the Project Manager and the project management team and reports to the Project Manager. The provision of a Project Support is optional.

The following is a suggested list of tasks:
*   Setting up and maintaining project files;
*   Establishing document control procedures;
*   Collecting actual data and forecasts;
*   Updating plans;
*   Assisting with the compilation of plans and reports;
*   Administering and assisting with Project Board meetings;
*   Administering and assisting with quality activities;
*   Maintaining the Quality Register and archiving quality records;

- Maintaining any other logs and registers as delegated by the Project Manager;
- Administering configuration and change control procedures;
- Maintaining Configuration Items Records;
- Preparing the Product Status Account and configuration audits;
- Contributing expertise in use of specialist tools and techniques.

Appendix C
Example of product-based planning

Product breakdown structure for a Conference

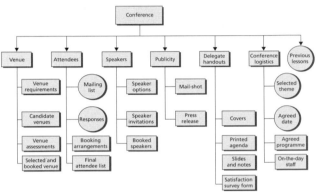

Fig. C.1 Example of product breakdown structure for a Conference (Source: Managing Successful Projects with PRINCE2, produced by OGC)

Product Description of venue requirements

- Identifier — 01
- Title — Venue requirements
- Purpose — To identify all the requirements that must be met by suitable venues for the conference
- Composition
  - Facilities required
  - Parking capacity
  - Attendees capacity
  - Accommodation capacity
- Derivation — PID, agreed date, previous lessons
- Format — Template of Purchase Department
- Development skills — Conference organizer
- Quality criteria
  - Specifications derived from input documents
  - Conditions of Purchase Department
- Quality tolerance — Quantities specified – 10%
- Quality method
  - Inspection of capacity
  - Quality review of facilities
- Quality skills
  - Familiar with conditions of Purchase Department
  - Familiar with organizing conferences
- Responsibilities
  - Producer: Peter
  - Reviewers: Angela and William
  - Approver: Head of Marketing & Sales

Product flow diagram for a Conference

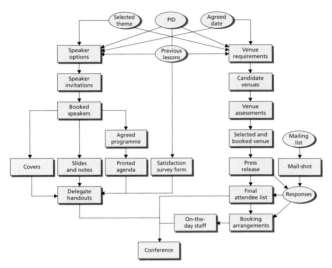

Fig. C2 Example of product flow diagram for a Conference (Based on OGC PRINCE2 material)

Appendix D
Glossary

The terms and descriptions in this Glossary are taken from: *Managing Successful Projects with PRINCE2®*, Fifth edition Crown Copyright, 2009.

accept (risk response)
A risk response to a threat where a conscious and deliberate decision is taken to retain the threat, having discerned that it is more economical to do so than to attempt a risk response action.

acceptance
The formal act of acknowledging that the project has met agreed acceptance criteria and thereby met the requirements of its stakeholders.

acceptance criteria
A prioritized list of criteria that the product must meet before the customer will accept it, i.e. measurable definitions of the attributes, required for the set of products to be acceptable to key stakeholders.

activity
A process, function or task that occurs over time, has recognizable results and is managed.

agile methods
Software development methods that apply the project approach of using time-boxed iterations where products are incrementally developed.

approval
Formal confirmation that a product is complete and meets its requirements as defined by its Product Description.

approver
The person or group who is identified as qualified and authorized to approve a product as being complete and fit for purpose.

assumption

A statement that is taken as being true for the purpose of planning, but which could change later.

assurance

All the systematic actions necessary to provide confidence that the target (system, process, organization, programme, project, outcome, benefit, capability, product, output, deliverable) is appropriate.

authority

The right to allocate resources and make decisions.

authorization

The point at which an authority is granted.

avoid (risk response)

A risk response to a threat where the threat either can no longer have an impact or can no longer happen.

baseline

Reference levels against which an entity is monitored and controlled.

benefit

The measurable improvement resulting from an outcome perceived as an advantage by one or more stakeholders.

Benefits Review Plan

A plan that defines how and when a measurement of the achievement of the project's benefits can be made.

benefits tolerance

The permissible deviation in the expected benefit that is allowed before the deviation needs to be escalated to the next level of management.

Business Case

The justification for an organizational activity (project) which typically contains costs, benefits, risks and timescales, and against which continuing viability is tested.

Change Authority

A person or group to which the Project Board may delegate responsibility for the consideration of requests for change and off-specifications.

change budget

The money allocated to Change Authority, available to be spent on authorized requests for change.

change control

The procedure that ensures that all changes that may affect the project's agreed objectives are identified, assessed and either approved, rejected or deferred.

checkpoint

A team-level, time-driven review of progress.

Checkpoint Report

A progress report of the information gathered at a checkpoint, which is given by a team to the Project Manager and which provides reporting data as defined in the Work Package.

closure notification

Advice from the Project Board to inform all stakeholders and the host sites that the project resources can be disbanded and support services, such as space, equipment and access, demobilized.

closure recommendation

A recommendation prepared by the Project Manager for the Project Board to send as a project closure notification when the board is satisfied that the project can be closed.

Communication Management Strategy

A description of the means and frequency of communication between the project and the project´s stakeholders.

concession

An off-specification that is accepted by the Project Board without corrective actions.

configuration item

An entity that is subject to configuration management (product, part of product or set of products in a release).

Configuration Item Record

A record that describes the status, version and variant of a configuration item, and any details of important relationships between them.

configuration management

Technical and administrative activities concerned with the creation, maintenance and controlled change of a configuration throughout the life of a product.

Configuration Management Strategy

A description of how and by whom the project's products will be controlled and protected.

configuration management system

The set of processes, tools and databases used to manage configuration data.

constraints

The restrictions or limitations the project is bound by.

contingency

Something that is held in reserve, typically to handle time and cost variances, or risks.

corrective action

A set of actions to resolve a tolerance threat to a plan's tolerances or a defect in a product.

cost tolerance

The permissible deviation in a plan's cost that is allowed before the deviation needs to be escalated to the next level of management.

customer

The person or group who commissioned the work and will benefit from the end results.

customer's quality expectations

A statement about the quality expected from the project product, captured in the Project Product Description.

Daily Log

Used to record the problems/concerns that can be handled by the Project Manager informally.

deliverable

See *output*.

dis-benefit

An outcome that is perceived as negative by one or more stakeholders.

DSDM Atern

An agile project delivery framework developed and owned by the DSDM consortium.

embedding (PRINCE2)

What an organization needs to do to adopt PRINCE2 as its corporate project management method.

End Project Report

A report given by Project Manager to the Project Board, that confirms the handover of all products and provides an updated Business Case and an assessment of how well the project has done against the Project Initiation Documentation.

end stage assessment

The review by the Project Board and Project Manager of the End Stage Report to decide whether to approve the next Stage Plan.

End Stage Report

A report given by Project Manager to the Project Board at the end of each management stage of the project.

enhance (risk response)

A risk response to an opportunity where proactive actions are taken to address both the probability of the event occurring and the impact of the event should it occur.

event-driven control

A control that takes place when a specific event occurs.

exception

A situation where it can be forecast that there will be a deviation beyond the tolerance levels, agreed between Project Manager and Project Board (or between Project Board and corporate or programme management).

exception assessment

A review by the Project Board to approve (or reject) an Exception Plan.

Exception Plan

A plan that often follows an Exception Report.

Exception Report

A description of the exception situation, its impact, options, recommendation and impact of the recommendation.

Executive

The single individual with overall responsibility for ensuring that a project meets its objectives and delivers the projected benefits.

exploit (risk response)

A risk response to an opportunity by seizing the opportunity to ensure that it will happen and the impact will be realized.

fallback (risk response)

A risk response to a threat by putting in place a fallback plan for the actions that will be taken to reduce the impact of the threat should the risk occur.

follow-on action recommendations

Recommended actions related to unfinished work, ongoing issues and risks, and any other activities needed to take a product to the next phase of its life.

governance (corporate)

The ongoing activity of maintaining a sound system of internal control by which the directors and officers of an organization ensure that effective management systems, including financial monitoring and control systems, have been put in place to protect assets, earning capacity and the reputation of the organization.

governance (project)

Those areas of corporate governance that are specifically related to project activities.

handover

The transfer of ownership of a set of products to the respective user(s).

Highlight Report

A time-driven report from the Project Manager to the Project Board on stage progress.

Impact (of risk)

The result of a particular threat or opportunity actually occurring, or the anticipation of such a result.

inherent risk

The exposure arising from a specific risk before any action has been taken to manage it.

initiation stage

The period from when the Project Board authorizes initiation to when they authorize the project (or decide not go ahead with the project).

issue

A relevant event that has happened, was not planned and requires management action.

Issue Register

A register used to capture and maintain information on of the issues that are being managed formally.

Issue Report

A report containing the description, impact assessment and recommendations for a request for change, off-specification or a problem/concern.

Lessons Log

An informal repository for lessons that apply to this project or future projects.

Lessons Report

A report that documents any lessons that can be usefully applied to other projects.

logs

Informal repositories managed by the Project Manager that do not require any agreement by the Project Board on their format and composition.

management product

A product that will be required as part of managing the project and establishing and maintaining quality.

management stage

The section of a project that the Project Manager is managing on behalf of the Project Board at any one time, at the end of which the Project Board will wish to review progress to date, the state of the Project Plan, the Business Case and risks, and the next Stage Plan in order to decide whether to continue with the project.

milestone

A significant event in a plan's schedule, such as completion of key Work Packages, a technical stage, or a management stage.

off-specification

Something that should be provided by the project, but currently it is not (or is forecast not to be) provided.

Operational and maintenance acceptance
A specific type of acceptance by the person or group who will support the product once it is handed over into the operational environment.

outcome
The result of change normally affecting real-world behaviour and/or circumstances.

output
A specialist product that is handed over to a user(s).

performance targets
A plan's goals for time, cost, quality, scope, benefits and risks.

plan
A detailed proposal for doing or achieving something which specifies the what, when, how and by whom.

planned closure
The PRINCE2 activity to close a project.

portfolio
All the programmes and stand-alone projects being undertaken by an organization, group of organizations, or an organizational unit.

premature closure
The PRINCE2 activity to close a project before its planned closure.

prerequisites (plan)
Any fundamental aspects that must be in place, and remain in place for a plan to succeed.

PRINCE2 principles
The guiding obligations for good project management practice that form the basis of a project being managed using PRINCE2.

probability

The evaluated likelihood of a particular threat or opportunity actually happening, including a consideration of the frequency with which it may arise.

problem/concern

A type of issue that the Project Manager needs to resolve or escalate.

procedure

A series of actions for a specific aspect of project management established specifically for the project, e.g. a risk management procedure.

process

A structured set of activities designed to accomplish a specific objective.

producer

The person or group responsible for developing a product.

product

An input or an output, whether tangible or intangible, that can be described in advance, created and tested.

product breakdown structure

A hierarchy of all the products to be produced during a plan.

product checklist

A list of the major products of a plan, plus key dates in their delivery.

Product Description

A description of a product's purpose, composition, derivation and quality criteria.

product flow diagram

A diagram showing the sequence in their production and interdependencies of the products listed in the product breakdown structure.

Product Status Account

A report on the status of products.

product-based planning
A technique leading to a comprehensive plan based on the creation and delivery of required outputs.

programme
A temporary flexible organization structure created to coordinate, direct and oversee the implementation of a set of related projects and activities in order to deliver outcomes and benefits related the organization's strategic objectives.

project
A temporary organization that is created for the purpose of delivering one or more business products according to an agreed Business Case.

project approach
A description of the way in which the work of the project is to be approached.

Project Assurance
The Project Board's responsibilities to assure itself that the project is being conducted correctly.

project authorization notification
Advice from the Project Board to inform the stakeholders and the host sites that the project has been authorized and to request any necessary logistical support sufficient for the duration of the project.

Project Brief
A statement that describes the purpose, cost, time and performance requirements, and constraints for a project.

Project Initiation Documentation
A logical set of documents that brings together the key information needed to start the project on a sound basis and that conveys the information to all concerned with the project.

project initiation notification
Advice from the Project Board to inform all stakeholders and the host sites the project is being initiated and to request any necessary logistical support sufficient for the initiation stage.

project lifecycle
The period from the start-up of a project to the acceptance of the project product.

project management
The planning, delegation, monitoring and control of all aspects of the project, and the motivation of those involved, to achieve the project objectives within the expected performance targets for time, cost, quality, scope, benefits and risks.

project management team
The entire management structure of the Project Board and Project Manager, plus any Team Manager, Project Assurance and Project Support roles.

project management team structure
An organization chart showing the people assigned to the project management team, roles to be used, and their delegation and reporting relationships.

Project Manager
The person given the authority and responsibility to manage the project on a day-to-day basis to deliver the required products within the constraints agreed with the Project Board.

project mandate
An external product generated by the authority commissioning the project that forms the trigger for Starting up a Project.

project office
A temporary office set up to support the delivery of a specific change initiative being delivered as a project.

Project Plan

A high-level plan showing the major products of the project, when they will be delivered and at what cost.

project product

What the project must deliver in order to gain acceptance.

Project Product Description

A special type of Product Description used to gain agreement from the user on the project's scope and requirements, to define the customer's quality expectations, and to define the acceptance criteria for the project.

Project Support

An administrative role in the project management team.

proximity (of risk)

The time factor of risk i.e. when the risk may occur.

quality

The totality of features and inherent or assigned characteristics of a product, person, process, service and/or system that bears on its ability to show that it meets expectations or stated needs, requirements or specifications.

quality assurance

An independent check that products will be fit for purpose or meet requirements.

quality control

The process of monitoring specific project results to determine whether they comply with relevant standards and of indentifying ways to eliminate causes of unsatisfactory performance.

quality criteria

A description of the quality specification that the product must meet, and the quality measurements that will be applied by those inspecting the finished product.

quality inspection
A systematic, structured assessment of a product carried out by two or more carefully selected people in a planned, documented and organized fashion.

quality management
The coordinated activities to direct and control an organization with regard to quality.

Quality Management Strategy
A strategy defining the quality techniques and standards to be applied, and the various responsibilities for achieving the required quality levels, during a project.

quality management system
The complete set of quality standards, procedures and responsibilities for a site or organization.

quality records
Evidence kept to demonstrate that the required quality assurance and quality control activities have been carried out.

Quality Register
A register containing summary details of all planned and completed quality activities.

quality review
See *quality inspection*.

quality review technique
A quality inspection technique with defined roles and a specific structure.

quality tolerance
The tolerance identified for a product for a quality criterion defining an acceptable range of values.

records
Dynamic management products that maintain information regarding project progress.

reduce (risk response)

A response to a risk where proactive actions are taken to reduce the probability of the event occurring by performing some form of control, and/or reduce the impact of the event should it occur.

registers

Formal repositories managed by the Project Manager that require agreement by the Project Board on their format, composition and use.

reject (risk response)

A response to a risk (opportunity) where a conscious and deliberate decision is taken not to exploit or enhance an opportunity, having discerned that it is more economical to do so than to attempt a risk response action.

release

The set of products in a handover.

reports

Management products providing a snapshot of the status on certain aspects of the project.

request for change

A proposal for a change to a baseline.

residual risk

The risk remaining after the risk response has been applied.

reviewer

A person or group independent of the producer who assesses whether a product meets its requirements as defined in its Product Description.

risk

An uncertain event or set of events that, should it occur, will have an effect on the achievement of objectives.

risk actionee

A nominated owner of an action to address a risk.

risk appetite

An organization's unique attitude towards risk taking that in turn dictates the amount of risk that it considers is acceptable.

risk estimation

The estimation of probability and impact of an individual risk, taking into account predetermined standards, target risk levels, interdependencies and other relevant factors.

risk evaluation

The process of understanding the net effect of the identified threats and opportunities on an activity when aggregated together.

risk management

The systematic application of principles, approaches and processes to the tasks of identifying and assessing risks, and then planning and implementing risk responses.

Risk Management Strategy

A strategy describing the goals of applying risk management, as well as the procedure that will be adopted, roles and responsibilities, risk tolerances, the timing of risk management interventions, the tools and techniques that will be used, and the reporting requirements.

risk owner

A named individual who is responsible for the management, monitoring and control of all aspects of a particular risk, assigned to them, including the implementation of the selected responses to address the threats or maximize the opportunities.

risk profile

A description of the types of risk that are faced by an organization and its exposure to those risks.

Risk Register

A record of identified risks relating to an initiative, including their status and history.

risk response

Actions that may be taken to bring a situation to a level where exposure to risk is acceptable to the organization.

risk tolerance

The threshold levels of risk exposure which, when exceeded, will trigger an Exception Report to bring the situation to the attention of the Project Board.

schedule

Graphical representation of a plan, typically describing a sequence of tasks, together with resource allocations, which collectively deliver the plan.

Scope

For a plan, the sum total of its products and the extent of their requirements.

scope tolerance

The permissible deviation in a plan's scope that is allowed before the deviation needs to be escalated to the next level of management.

Senior Responsible Owner (SRO)

A UK government term for the individual responsible for ensuring that a project or programme of change meets its objectives and delivers the projected benefits.

Senior Supplier

The Project Board role that provides knowledge and experience of the main discipline(s) involved in the production of the project's deliverables.

Senior User

The Project Board role accountable for ensuring that user needs are specified correctly and that the solution meets those needs.

share (risk response)
A risk response to either a threat or an opportunity through the application of a pain/gain formula: both parties share the gain if the cost is less than the cost plan; and both share the pain if the cost plan is exceeded.

specialist product
A product whose development is the subject of the plan.

sponsor
The main driving force behind a programme or project.

stage
See management stage or technical stage.

Stage Plan
A detailed plan used as the basis for project management control throughout a stage.

stakeholder
Any individual, group or organization that can affect, be affected by, or perceive itself to be affected by an initiative (programme, project, activity, risk).

start-up
The pre-project activities undertaken by the Executive and the Project Manager to produce the outline Business Case, Project Brief and Initiation Stage Plan.

strategy
An approach or line to take, designed to achieve a long-term aim.

supplier
The person, group or groups responsible for the supply of the project's specialist products.

tailoring

The appropriate use of PRINCE2 on any given project, ensuring that there is the correct amount of planning, control, governance and use of the processes and themes.

Team Manager

The person responsible for the production of those products allocated by the Project Manager (as defined in the Work Package) to an appropriate quality, timescale and at a cost acceptable to the Project Board.

Team Plan

An optional level of plan used as a basis for team management control when executing Work Packages.

technical stage

A method of grouping work together by the set of techniques used, or the products created.

theme

An aspect of project management that needs be continually addressed, and that requires specific treatment for the PRINCE2 processes to be effective.

time tolerance

The permissible deviation in a plan's time that is allowed before the deviation needs to be escalated to the next level of management.

time-driven control

A management control that is periodic in nature, to enable the next higher authority to monitor progress.

tolerance

The permissible deviation above and below a plan's target for time and cost (but also possible for scope, quality, benefits and risks) without escalating the deviation to the next level of management.

transfer (risk response)
A response to a threat where a third party takes on responsibility for some of the financial impact of the threat.

trigger
An event or decision that triggers a PRINCE2 process.

user
The person or group who will use one or more of the project's products.

user acceptance
A specific type of acceptance by the person or group who will use the product once it is handed over into the operational environment.

variant
A variation on a baselined product.

version
A specific baseline of a product.

waterfall method
A development approach that is linear and sequential with distinct goals for each phase of development.

Work Package
The set of information relevant to the creation of one or more products.

Appendix E
Governance

Project management governance covers those areas related to project activities. Effective project management governance ensures that corporate management and other stakeholders are well informed and that the project portfolio will align with the organization's objectives, will be delivered efficiently and is sustainable. Table E.1 shows the degree to which PRINCE2 addresses the APM governance principles.

Governance of project management principles	Is this governance principle addressed by PRINCE2?
The Board is responsible for project management governance.	The main board of corporate management is not addressed by PRINCE2.
The roles, responsibilities and performance criteria for project management governance are clearly defined.	The role descriptions within PRINCE2 are clear on this subject, however corporate management is not addressed, therefore the principle is partially addressed.
Disciplined governance arrangements are applied throughout the project lifecycle.	Fully addressed.
Relationship is demonstrated between overall business strategy and project portfolio.	Partially through the Business Case. PRINCE2 does not address project portfolio.
Projects have an approved plan containing decision points with Business Case reviews and approvals. Decisions made are recorded and communicated.	Fully addressed.
Members of delegated authorization bodies have sufficient representation, competence, authority and resources to be able to make the right decisions.	Partially addressed because PRINCE2 has a framework for effective delegation, though it does not describe the competencies of project personnel involved.
The Business Case is supported by adequate information providing a basis for making authorization decisions.	Fully addressed.
The board decides when independent scrutiny is required and implements it accordingly.	Partially addressed because PRINCE2 recommends independent corporate or programme management scrutiny as a part of Project Assurance.
Criteria for reporting project status and the escalation of issues and risks to the required levels are clearly defined.	Fully addressed.

Governance of project management principles	Is this governance principle addressed by PRINCE2?
The organization fosters a culture of improvement and an (internal) openness to project information.	Partially addressed by the management-by-exception and assurance responsibilities.
Stakeholders are engaged at the right level according to their importance.	Fully addressed.

Table E.1 APM Governance principles and PRINCE2 (Source: *Directing Change: A Guide to Governance of Project Management*, APM Governance SIG. © Association for Project Management, 2004. Reproduced with permission)

Appendix F
Organizations

APMG International Offices

APMG-UK – www.apmgroup.co.uk
APMG-Benelux – www.apmg-benelux.com
APMG-China – www.apmg-china.com
APMG-Deutschland – www.apmg-deutschland.com
APMG-Scandinavia – www.apmg-scandinavia.com
APMG-US – www.apmg-us.com
APMG-Australasia - www.apmg-australasia.com

Best Practice User Group UK – www.usergroup.org.uk
PRINCE User Group Netherlands – www.pugnl.nl
PRINCE User Group Germany – www.prince2-deutschland.de

Other project management organizations
IPMA – www.ipma.ch
APM – www.apm.org.uk
PMI – www.pmi.org

Appendix G
References

1. *Managing Successful Projects with PRINCE2™*, Fifth edition, © Crown copyright 2009, TSO
2. *Directing Successful Projects with PRINCE2™*, First edition, © Crown copyright 2009, TSO

About the authors

Bert Hedeman is a senior project and programme manager and managing partner of Insights International BV. Bert is an accredited PRINCE2 and MSP trainer and co-author of the books 'Project Management based on PRINCE2' and 'Programme Management based on MSP'. Since 1995, Bert has also been an accredited assessor for IPMA.

Ron Seegers is a senior project management trainer and PRINCE2 accredited trainer. He has worked in projects as project manager using PRINCE2.

Ron has helped organizations to adapt and adopt PRINCE2. He is experienced in conducting PRINCE2 in the Dutch, English and German language.

Not only as a trainer but also as coach, he empowers people to use PRINCE2 the right way with the right skills. Ron owns 'Projectmeester', a training and coaching company and is board member of the Dutch PRINCE User Group (www.PUGnl.nl).